GMAT Verbal 99%ile

Mitsubishi's Japanese Language Learning
Experiment on an Indian

Kamal Sinha

LEGAL MATTERS

Any conjecture in this book about Mitsubishi Electric's thinking and motive is what a reasonable person will arrive at given the facts that the author had access to. In case you plan to communicate to him regarding this matter or any other legal concerns, please send him an email at legal@kamalsinha.com.

Thanks to

Attorney Satoshi Murata,

Kaoru and

my late mother

Write to me:

mitsubishi@kamalsinha.com

Visit my site: www.kamalsinha.com

Names in the book: Yui and Emma are fictitious names.

Table of Contents

Table of Contents (continued)

Foreword

Historically Japan has been reluctant to use foreign-born labor which some subscribe to its xenophobia but in recent years, Japanese multinationals have started coming to India in increasing numbers for the purpose of hiring Indians. Concerning relation between Japan and India, we know the drill from our textbooks and mass media - we are both Asians; they sacrificed their lives for keeping Asia for Asians, they had high regards for Netaji Bose and tried to help him overthrow British rule in India; they are Buddhists and respect India for its origin; their prime minister Mr. Abe follows only 3 people on twitter and one of them is Mr. Modi; they gave us bullet trains for almost free; we both have a common adversary in China. OMG! We are the same people separated by a few thousands of miles.

A few years ago I happened to meet the Dean of recruitment of IIT, Bombay, in USA. He appeared elated by his perception that IITB was held in such high regard by foreign multinationals. He mentioned the Mitsubishi group in particular. Seemed like over a dozen or so Mitsubishi CEO's had visited IITB campus together recently and they were so impressed with IITB graduates that he was told that they wanted them to become CEO's of Mitsubishi companies in future. Really impressive!

Amid all this euphoria concerning India and Japan's mutual relationship, I am a little reluctant to tell my story. It is about how 30 years ago; Mitsubishi Electric in Japan hired me from USA, an IITian, for the purpose of conduct-

1

ing an experiment on me to observe how fast I could learn the Japanese language by immersing me in Japanese environment, of course without any training or outside help. .

Court documents related to my lawsuit in Japan will be initially placed at my site kamalsinha.com, and later I will get them translated and commented on by scholars.

I studied at IIT, Bombay batch of 1978, where among others, Mr. Nandan Nilekani and Mr. Manohar Parrikar were there, and who don't need any introduction. I need some introduction though. Mundane details about me can be found at the beginning Pre-Recruitment chapter.

Kamal Sinha

June, 2016

Introduction

Japan, while continuing with its stronghold on the world market is still the third largest economy of the world, with technological leadership in many areas but is relatively lagging behind when it comes to software development. While the US, the number one economy has benefited tremendously from an influx of software professionals, Japan has had not much luck in this regard.

If one looks for the reasons, one of the biggest issues Japan faces is the language barrier. Japanese companies conduct their business naturally in Japanese language. Foreigners cannot be an integral part of their workplace unless they are reasonably fluent in Japanese. Written Japanese, which mainly consists of *kanjis*, the adopted Chinese characters, is particularly difficult to master. One needs to learn over 2,000 *kanjis* (there are over 50,000) in order to function adequately in written Japanese. (It took me a few thousand hours to learn these *kanjis* and I forgot half of it the instant my proficiency test ended!). And then there are *hiragana* and *katakana*, two simpler scripts but nevertheless adding to the complexity of the language. Most foreigners without prior exposure to Chinese characters limit themselves to learning these two scripts. However, this won't suffice in the Japanese business world where reasonable mastery of *kanjis* is a required skill.

Mitsubishi Electric in 1988 and earlier was in deep waters. Even though it was a major company of the prestigious Mitsubishi group, and manufactured some high quality electrical equipment like the big screen TV's, because of a few past business failures it was not a big name in the computer industry and therefore was not able to attract graduates of top universities to its computer works. On top of that, the declining birth rates, as is normal in the developed world but more so in Japan, resulted in fewer potentially available domestic workers (for the present and future) was adding to their grief. Importing foreign labor (as was and has always been the case in USA), was being considered.

As a pilot study, it was planning to hire a few graduates from top-ranked schools, in the US and the UK, to bring them to Japan, keep them in employment for five years or so, and observe how they adopt to the Japanese workplace. It was useful in some limited aspects but the real focus for them was India which had been the world's biggest supplier of software personnel. While top graduates of developed countries tended to stay back home, Indian graduates of its top technical schools like the IIT's opted mainly for migrating to the developed world, especially the US. Among the ones who chose to stay in India or couldn't go abroad, working for a western multinational in India was often the preferred career path. Japan in general was absent from their radar screen.

Thanks to their education system where English was emphasized, most technical Indians developed good proficiency in the English language and this made them desired employees in the English-speaking developed countries, provided they had other skills and Indians too preferred those countries because of the ease of adjustment.

Ideal situation for the Japanese would have been to change the education system in India to Japanese-language-based but that didn't seem likely. Urban Indians were mostly multilingual though and Indians have shown a penchant for learning foreign languages like English. Some, like the ones from English-medium private schools have English-language proficiency that exceeds that of the typical native English speakers. I have met quite a few of them at IIT. What if the technical workers from India, ones with high verbal aptitude, were hired and brought to Japan, put in an immersive Japanese language environment, and through subtle and not-so-subtle pressure tactics were forced to learn the Japanese language – both spoken and written – to a decent level as soon as possible, say one year, while them remaining productive in their assigned work, language-related issues could be minimized. A pilot study was desirable.

In 1988, Japan was on a roll with its stock markets surging (Nikkei index reached its peak of 39,957 on December 29, 1989, just a few weeks after I joined Mitsubishi Electric in August of 1989.) It was able to compete with the US in most technical fields with noticeable exception being computer software where it lagged behind seriously. Computer software was the emerging technology pivotal to deciding which country was going to be the leader of the next century and beyond. If this pilot study were a success who knows Japan could have started thinking of hiring Indians by planeloads or shiploads and could then even compete with USA for dominance. What a contrast from the situation nowadays when some experts are forecasting a collapse of the Japanese economy not too far in future. As a layman though, I am much more positive on Japan.

As a serendipity my resume made it to them at that time and it had what the company was exactly looking for its pilot study. I was hired to be the subject of the language experiment. It was one of the biggest hiring in the company's history with about 16 senior executives signing the papers to hire me. The recruitment and experiment were connived and executed with utmost care like anything Mitsubishi group companies are known for.

In its excitement to hire me, the company made a few serious mistakes that showed its true nature and what they really thought of Indians. A rare racial discrimination lawsuit by me in Japanese courts forced them to expose their hands further.

Pre-Recruitment

Hi, I am Kamal Sinha and I am from Bihar. Bihar is the state where the Buddha received his enlightenment and King Ashoka sent emissaries to countries like China for the spread of his teachings. I was born near Nalanda, site of ancient Buddhist University in Bihar and spent my childhood in Ichapore in West Bengal. Right after my high school education from Kendriya Vidyalaya (Central School), Barrackpore I joined IIT, Bombay at the age of 16 in the department of electrical engineering in 1973. After working for Larsen & Toubro in Mumbai and Chennai altogether for about three years I went to the US in 1981 to pursue an MBA and later MS in computer science both from Southern Illinois University at Carbondale. In the meantime, I supported myself financially through fellowships and later graduate assistantships.

I joined University of Tennessee at Martin starting Fall 1984 as an assistant professor teaching computer science courses to undergraduate students. Martin was one of the three campuses of the university, primarily serving undergraduates and had about 5,000 students. It was a dead-end job with virtually no potential career growth. The job required teaching 3-4 basic courses and grading them. Since it was difficult to find American citizens or green card holders to apply for such a job, it made the task of getting labor certification easier which led to green card later. Many students on visas accepted such jobs and left after acquiring their green cards. Getting a green card took less than two years normally.

While studying at Southern Illinois University I met a gentleman, Khurshid from Bangladesh. He was studying to become an English teacher and was very friendly with all and was popular with the Japanese students there. They seemed very friendly though most of them spoke little English. Hearing about them from Khurshid, who later went to Japan, piqued my interest in knowing more about the Japanese people.

While in my second year teaching at the university, in 1985 I enrolled in a simple, conversation Japanese course offered there. I had many Japanese students enrolled in my courses, they didn't seem to be very comfortable speaking English but were friendly towards me though shy. I thought knowing a litter conversational Japanese would help me understand them better.

Yui, a graduate student from Japan, was teaching that conversational Japanese course, and one thing led to another, and I started dating her. At first I was fascinated by her shy and introvert nature, and I knew that Japanese women are traditionally strong but I was bothered by her apparent lack of interest in my family - for example I doubt she ever asked me how many siblings I had. She also didn't show any interest in my career plans but it didn't bother me that much.

In a short time, she started claiming that she loved me. I told her that I didn't love her but was willing to try. In the summer of 1986, about one year from our first meeting, she had to go back to Japan, for good. She was from a remote town in Japan, and wanted to stay in Japan, to take care of her parents. Her father was a small businessman and apparently was well-off. She wanted me to come to Japan and explore the idea of marrying her and living there.

8

Before going to the US, all the material I had read about in India about Japan was very positive. They were a hard working race and tried to liberate India and other Asian countries from Western Colonialism and paid a heavy price for that by having atom bombs dropped on them. These racist Westerners! Nowhere did I read about them destroying millions of Asian lives by murdering and raping them. In the US, I read many newspaper articles about those atrocities, how they considered themselves to be superior to other Asians and how Chinese and Koreans who lived in Japan were treated very badly, and things like that. And many lawsuits against Mitsubishi and other big companies for wartime atrocities made it to the newspapers often.

I told her that I had recently read very bad things about Japan - its rampant racism and incessant discrimination that Asian population of Chinese and Korean ancestry faced daily and the dirty account of World War 2 that I didn't know about while in India. And the question of job - never heard of good jobs offered in Japan to non-Caucasian foreigners. She assured me that Japan was more open-minded than reported. I told her since my green card is expected soon, I will visit Japan after that to see things by myself, probably live and explore Tokyo for a short while, and then decide what to do next. She agreed.

She started writing to me - almost every week. Rarely, we also talked on phone. Her letters were very constrained and while friendly lacked romantic warmth. Time was passing by.

After a while things didn't look so promising and I wanted to break up with Yui but thought that breaking up in person was the polite thing to do. I decided to wait till I go to Japan after getting my US green card and at least give our relationship a try and talk to her about a lot of things. She looked emotionally fragile and some comments from her made me nervous.

Unfortunately, the green card process was delayed unnecessarily thanks to the incompetence of my first lawyer. Days turned into months and years. Two years had nearly passed. It was mid-1988, when things started moving fast.

A few months prior I had started subscribing to an animal rights magazine - Animals' Agenda - and through its Vege-Dates service I had met Emma towards the end of 1987. [**Exhibit A1**]

She lived in conservative south but was vegetarian like me, very liberal and well-read. We hit it off well. We had some minor differences but in a way she was a great match for me. We lived far away, a few hundred miles away, that prevented our meeting often, we met once in a few months, and I think that affected our relationship. I told her about Yui and she told me to make my own decision.

Marrying Emma would have resulted in a green card being granted much quickly but I wanted to get my green card on my own. In case I didn't get the green card, there was India and many other countries like the Canada, Australia which were vying for young talented workers like me. Some people do get married for their green card and are content to live their lives that way but that was not me. In Japan, I heard about a foreigner married to a Japanese woman who was working for a large company. He got fed up of working for that company but apparently his Japanese wife used to throw cold water on him in the mornings to force him to go to work. Ouch! In the US, I came across an Indian person who married an Indian-American woman just for the green card. She used to abuse him and used to remind him often that everything he was in life was because of her. They eventually got divorced but not before he turned into an alcoholic. Incidentally, since he got divorced before the probationary period he didn't get his green card too. Last time I saw him around 2012 when he was assured by a lawyer that he deserved a green card based on that abusive marriage. I could go on and on but it's time to move on with my story.

In March/April 1988, I first heard from Yui who mentioned her mother wondering when I would be coming to Japan. Very soon, she started demanding that I quit everything in the US and come to Japan for 'love' which in turn led to our frequent fights. At first, I didn't understand what this 'love' meant. I surely didn't love her and I was not sure about her love too. I think her age and her mother's comments added to her desperation. Then my appeal for a third petition approval in front of the Board of Immigration, Washington D.C. was under way and chances of approval of my petition looked excellent. I was not going to jeopardize that after fighting for it for 4 years in turn for a country which I didn't think I wanted to live in. We continued fighting over phone for a few weeks but I refused to come to Japan. She wrote me a long letter. **[Exhibit B]**

I had received approval of my appeal for the third petition by then **[Exhibit C]** and informed Yui that I will get my green card within 6 months and will be in Japan by December (of 1988) even though I thought that the Summer of 1989 would be the earliest I will be in Japan and I was in no hurry to go there. I thought I could then talk to her in person and decide on our future plans, including any breakup. I had to do it at least for her because she had waited for such a long time for me and she seemed emotionally vulnerable.

If I was unable to come to Japan at that time, she wanted a copy of my resume so that she could arrange for interviews so that when I did land, I wouldn't have to waste time and straight away go for interviews. I didn't like it, losing control of the job search process, and thought of it as a silly and futile idea and resisted that but saw a bright light. I was certain that she would not be able to arrange a single interview, which meant convincing her that there were no jobs for me in Japan, and making the task of breaking up and leaving Japan after a brief meeting a breeze.

I sent her copies of my resume [**Exhibit D**] and explained to her to apply for only financial jobs and not to any computer related jobs which I was not interested in but many employers wanted mysteriously to put Indians in. She agreed. I assumed that she would apply to the US based companies, and since now the green card was almost certain and I was definitely going to Japan only after receiving it, put 'Permanent Resident' in the personal section of the resume. I could have written "Pending Permanent Residency" or "Expecting Permanent Residency soon" but for parsimonious use of the phrase, I settled on plain 'Permanent Resident.' At the time of any potential interview in Japan that would be true.

Things were looking up. I had worked hard for my actuarial, and investment exams and the future looked bright. There was a shortage of actuaries, especially ones with excellent abilities in finance. About 500 actuaries got

Society of Actuaries associate designation each year after passing very rigorous exams. Most applicants failed exams multiple times and made it through sheer perseverance. My test scores were quite good and I passed all the associate ship exams in my first attempt.

A couple of weeks later, I received a letter [**Exhibit E1**][**Exhibit E2**] from Yui, informing me that Mitsubishi Electric wanted to hire me for a permanent job in their computer works for doing system engineering work. For me it was a nightmarish scenario – a job I absolutely didn't want but I was not too worried since I thought I would be stalling them soon. I wondered though what they saw in my resume for them to decide to hire me.

Recruitment

Yui's father, a small businessman perhaps not much educated, saw the Mitsubishi Electric's job ad in for system engineers in a Japanese newspaper [**Exhibit F**] and thought that it would be a good job for me and told Yui about it. Two days later, she applied for the job, forwarding my resume for 'Investment Analyst' [**Exhibit D**] for 'system engineering' job, filled out a short application form, and in the section for the relationship of the person filling out the form to the applicant mentioned 'fiancée' and in the next section mentioned that 'after getting married planned to live in Japan.' [**Exhibit G**]

This was all done without my knowledge. This application resulted in one of the biggest recruitment in the company's history but not for the reasons one would normally expect.

Hiring Rationale

There were no skills matching between the job ad and my resume. My job objective was 'Investment Analyst' and the entire resume was dedicated to justifying that by mentioning my high quantitative aptitude, and passing various CFA, CFP and actuarial exams. I did have a MS in computer science but my most recent experience - teaching basic programming courses to undergraduates in a small teaching institution didn't add to my skill set and in fact had rusted the skills I already had prior to joining that job. (In technical areas like computer science, 4-5 years of such experience without any apparent attempt to improve the skills leads to almost obsolescence.) Any other company would have summarily dismissed my resume.

At that time Mitsubishi Electric was thinking of the idea of fulfilling labor shortage for computer professionals by importing workers. India was the obvious choice. Their main concern was their Japanese-language skills. How would they function in the company where the language of communication was Japanese, both verbal and written? Giving them Japanese-language training was a simple answer but it was very expensive in terms of time and money. Instead, it would be nice for them to learn Japanese language "naturally" that is by immersing them in Japanese-language at workplace, talking to them in Japanese language, asking them to write reports in Japanese-language, using subtle and not-so-subtle tactics to make them learn faster by spending more time in studying Japanese-language. Their guess was that ideally within a year or so these workers from India should be able to reach at least a functional level in Japanese-language.

However, before that my resume was staring them on their faces and one group of keywords that popped out from that resume consisting of useless information was **"GMAT Verbal: 99%."** Such scores are as rare as a unicorn in English-language-challenged Japan and they thought it would be nice if they could bring me to the computer works and use me as a pilot study to determine how much Japanese a person of my superior language-skills could possibly learn in a year with absolutely no help.

Jealousy

Also, it was the matter of jealousy. Just like a beauty-challenged jealous person might love to spill acid on a beautiful person, verbally-challenged Mitsubishi Electric executives would have been tempted to do something similar to me. Mitsubishi has long prided itself on being superior to other Asians but my resume staring at them was a direct challenge to their beliefs. Not only in verbal skills, in quant skill too in which the Japanese took pride in their superiority (most international testing place them on or near-top in such skills) my resume was telling them that it was not likely that anyone in Mitsubishi or even Japan was better than me in that regard too. It must have been so humiliating being inferior to a lowly Indian! Later, when I was watching the wonderful movie Amadeus I was struck by the fact that even moderately gifted people feel so jealous of really gifted individuals like Mozart and stoop to unimaginable levels to destroy their lives. Let's face it - a language learning experiment on me was completely useless. It is like dropping atom bombs directly on people to test whether people survive them or not. They had experience with foreigners including Indians and knew how fast they had learned Japanese. They could have consulted experts about language learning. Or better still, could have provided Indians like me with some sort of Japanese language training. Instead, the language learning experiment though on surface was done for a business purpose but it had its roots perhaps in this deep-seated jealousy and its real purpose was to harass me for being someone they could never be. In verbally-challenged Mitsubishi Electric, I suffered because I was verbally-gifted, in the US the quant-challenged persons harassed me (details in my next book) because I was quant-gifted, a gifted person just can't seem to get a break. I guess jealousy is the dominant emotion when it comes to dealing with gifted people. I am so glad that I was not considered exceptionally handsome; otherwise I would also have to be on constant look outs for acid spills from every direction.

More on jealousy: Raising the idea that jealousy played a role in any decision is a big no-no. It opens up the person to ridicule by someone providing the evidence that the person is not-so-good and is just so full of it. I think at this very moment probably somebody is saying to himself, "What an egoist maligning the nicest people from Mitsubishi. I will show him." I have laid open my cards and I have only this to say, "bring it on."

A sad side story: A few years ago a video was making the rounds on internet. An 18-year old driving a convertible Porsche was behind a slow-moving Honda. After honking when the Honda car didn't yield, she decided to change lane to the slower lane and pass that car. Unfortunately, as she changed lanes, so did the Honda car driver to give her way at about the same time. Their cars touched, the Porsche overturned and her head scraped on the highway for quite a distance. Of course, she had a horrible death. Incidentally, someone took a video of it.

There were people thrilled with that video and posted mean, gloating comments. In my view, being jealous of a young woman able to drive an expensive car, those posters could only dream of driving instead driving their clunkers, was the driving factor. People remain no longer humans when jealousy strikes.

But back to the main narrative- a few roadblocks existed though. My resume mentioned that I was a Permanent Resident. It had to be taken care of.

U.S. Permanent Residency

The first time I met Mr. Satoshi Murata who became my attorney later, was when he heard that I am a permanent resident of the USA and have a lifetime employment with Mitsubishi Electric he looked very surprised and remarked that Japanese companies don't offer lifetime employment to green card holders. Later in court, while examining me the company lawyer produced a paper and asked me to identify that as the one I had submitted to the company, I scanned quickly for the phrase I was looking for - it hardly took less than 5 seconds - and I spotted it or rather spotted its absence from the place I had put it there and pointed out firmly that it was not my resume because 'Permanent Resident' was missing from that. Mitsubishi Electric had presented a fake resume in court!

You may wonder what is so special about the US permanent residency. It of course is valid in the US but in Japan for a Japanese company? There is a business protocol in Japanese companies - with few exceptions, citizens of developed world are treated different (means better) as compared to the citizens of developing countries like India and China. I think people familiar with middle-east employment practices will understand this particular job practice. Permanent citizens of USA are offered jobs similar to citizens of developed countries.

In my resume 'Permanent resident' was mentioned very prominently. However, Mitsubishi Electric after some analysis came to the conclusion that I was lying and was coming to Japan because I had failed in my bid to obtain a US green card.

How did they come to that erroneous conclusion which was pivotal to their decision to hire me? Mitsubishi Electric and other Mitsubishi group companies have many subsidiaries in the US they have sponsored many employees for green card and were aware of the process and its timeline. They knew that people joining a teaching institute like mine would ordinarily receive their green cards within two years and soon afterwards would leave for greener pastures to further their careers. In my case, after 4 academic years I was still at the university with at least one more term (actually one complete academic year) left there. In all likelihood, I was one of the unlucky few who had managed to have his green card application messed up and was instead coming to Japan. So why mention green card? To fool companies in Japan in thinking that I have a green card and get job offers offered to green card holders-meaning better jobs. Second one was to fool Yui that in spite of green card I was coming to Japan because of her and wanted to settle in Japan.

Their second hint was the application form filled by Yui. Why would somebody from India after going through the trouble to get the coveted green card be willing to come to Japan and settle down there? It didn't seem right.

Their third hint was the timing of the application. It seemed like I had difficulty getting a Japanese visa. If I had the green card, getting a Japanese visa wouldn't have been difficult at all and I would have been in Japan during the summer looking for jobs if that's what I wanted to do. At the outset, it looked like I was asking a Japanese woman to apply for jobs and she seemed to be doing so without much direction while I stayed in the US unable to enter Japan.

They could have directly asked me or Yui. It had its risks of alerting us by making me think of the connection between my US green card and the permanent job at Mitsubishi Electric. The risk was not worth it given the almost certainty of me not being a green card holder.

Cover Rationale

The company needed a plausible story in case unexpectedly things went wrong. The story was going to be simple:

I had no job skills but in the application form filled by Yui, she had indicated that I was engaged to her and I planned to marry her and live in Japan. So as a gesture of goodwill and to help a Japanese woman, Mitsubishi Electric decided to hire me as a permanent employee which is a job reserved usually for foreigners married to Japanese citizens and to provide me with some basic job training so that I could be employable in future. In return, I promised to marry Yui as soon as possible as per their Japanese employment "system" which was explained to me during my interview in the US. This was going to be their story and they were going to stick with it.

Comment: Mitsubishi Electric used some other rationales in the court for their actions. They were beyond ridiculous and I will talk about it or let you judge for yourself when I get the court documents translated from Japanese language.

Recruitment Plan

In reality, permanent job for foreigners is mostly for workers from developing countries like China and India which is tied to the condition of marriage to a Japanese citizen. Temporary jobs are given mostly to workers from developed countries and their situation is special with big houses, fat salaries, cushy jobs, you name it. Have you seen the movie Lost in Translation? To lure me, permanent job has to be sold as a 'pioneer' job and not like temporary job offered to Caucasian foreigners. Given Asians fear discrimination in Japan (and almost surely I suffered that in the US) repeat the mantra that I would be treated 'just like a Japanese.' Japanese language training could not be offered because it would be unfair to Japanese employees (remember the objective of the recruitment) because they don't get any language training. Instead, they fed me constant reminders that a comfortable job environment for me was being prepared because foreign workers without any Japanese language skills needed that in a Japanese workplace and for adjusting to the new way of life. And get Yui very much involved and become her best friend, first Mr. Kobayashi from the head office and then Mr. Urabe from computer works. They called and talked to her often because she was the main source of information about me and was going to be the recruitment agent for them and deliver me to them.

My comments: In Nagoya, the company had one Indian employee but I knew about him only much later after working for over one year when he came to me on company's behalf. He was married to a Japanese citizen. Japanese employees were getting English language training - at company premises. Absolutely no preparation was made for making workplace 'comfortable' for me. Everything was consistent with their plan for the experiment on me.

Recruitment in Action

My resume was for an Investment Analyst and the job ad was for 'system engineers.'

1. I got a letter from Yui. It said that Mitsubishi Electric was very much interested in hiring me and promised a comfortable workplace [Exhibit E1][Exhibit E2]. Seemed like they offered temporary jobs to other foreigners but had decided to give me a permanent job, treat me just like they would treat a Japanese person, and I would be a pioneer.

2. I talked to Yui. I didn't know how they decided to hire me for the job I absolutely didn't want and in a place and

company that was like serving a death sentence. She was excited though after talking to Mr. Kobayashi from head office and she asked me two questions she was asked to ask me:

1. Do I want to come to Japan?

2. Do I want to work for Mitsubishi Electric?

Stupid questions I thought. The fact that she had applied and was asked to ask me these questions could bias the answers heavily. I wonder why the company was asking through her and not directly me which would have resulted in totally different answers. And why offer a permanent job and not 1 or 2 year temporary job when they could clearly read that I have a US green card.

Comment: Company was testing how much Yui has influence over me because she was going to be the one to force me to sign their contract in future if I refused to sign it on my own..

3. Got a phone call from Yui. The company had hired me and was preparing a comfortable work environment for me. It seemed like somebody from the US was going to contact me to discuss the potential job assignment.

Comment: Seemed like a very fast recruitment process! What did they see in my resume? Why the company and Yui seemed to have become best friends? Is this a Japanese thing? I will have to stall them at least until I am in Japan was my first thought.

4. Got a call from Mr. Kawasaki, president of Mitsubishi Electronics America. He wanted me to come to Los Angeles for interview. I politely refused stating that my tight class

schedule does not allow it. He asked me about the nearest airport to me (Memphis) and called back a few hours later stating that he and his vice-president Mr. Kitahara have changed their flight from Pittsburg to Los Angeles to make an overnight stopover at Memphis.

5. I thought of using the excuse the car didn't start so that I don't have to see them but later relented as I thought Yui would come to know and start screaming on phone. I decided to let them know that I was interested in finance jobs only and will talk to any potential employer in Japan only.

6. I tried to avoid talking about job and instead indulged in small talk. First, I informed him that I was only interested in a finance job to which he answered 'we want to put you in financial software development.' He sounded fake but I didn't press him. I had no plans to meet the company in Japan so any talks were futile. Also informed him that only when I will go to Japan next summer, will meet with investment banks first and will talk to Mitsubishi Electric only then. Mr. Kawasaki kept quiet.

All of a sudden, he asked me 'tell me more about your fiancée, are you going to marry her?' I thought it was none of his business, but had read that Japanese companies ask such questions and instead of getting offended just smiling and politely answering was the correct protocol. I wondered what had Yui told them and would deal with her when I reached Japan. Didn't want to tell the truth that I don't want to marry her to strangers like him so just gave him a polite noncommittal answer to keep Mitsubishi Electric as last-option choice alive, if everything went wrong , wondering what they saw in my resume, "there is a very good chance but nothing is sure, he he he." I thought

24

if there is some condition like 'we want to make you the CEO of Mitsubishi Electric but you have to be married to a Japanese', he would announce then but he kept silent.

Suddenly he asked where I wanted to be in 5 years. I had thought of that and very poker-faced told him, "head of Indian subsidiary of some big multinational." He answered quickly, "you will have to leave after 5 years." That shocked me. I just nodded and said, "We can discuss at interview in Japan." I was willing to quit after 5 years if things went wrong and a suitable very generous severance package was worked out. But I was not going to work for them and it didn't matter. He also informed me about lack of vegetarian food in the company and the need for me to bring food from home to which I simply nodded my head because I was not going to work for them.

Then in a very sad voice Mr. Kawasaki told me that the company could not provide me with any Japanese language training since it would be unfair to the Japanese staff. It was surprising but I simply nodded my head.

He took out my resume and asked me to make any changes to it. 'Permanent Resident' was glaring at me and just below in my handwriting, I added a few other financial exams I had passed since I had emailed my resume to Yui.

Comment: I thought it would be the last I would have to deal with this company and that made me happy. I told Yui that I did badly in the interview. I reminded her to apply for investment banking jobs only and she started applying for those jobs.

7. A couple of weeks later, I got a call from Yui informing me that Mr. Kobayashi had called from the head office and

25

informed her that I would be transferred to the head office in 6 months. I considered that to be a confirmation of agreeing to my terms and a case of them having blinked first.

8. In November, Mr. Kawasaki called me asking if I could come to Japan in December to meet computer works executives to discuss my job responsibility. I curtly said 'No.'

Comment: I had told Mr. Kawasaki that I was coming to Japan in May/June 1989. I had told Yui that I would be coming in December 1988. The company was trying to determine when I was coming so that I could be hired before coming to Japan.

9. In December, I got a call from Yui. Computer works had asked her and her mother to visit computer works but asked her to ask for my permission first. This seemed very unusual and I told her not to go but Yui was not going to listen and made the visit. She had turned into a hysterical screaming person who wouldn't take no for an answer. Mr. Kobayashi had done his magic on her. Later, she called me telling me that during her visit to the Computer Works, she was asked by the company to select an apartment for me and she did, and to order a bed for me which she did. I was just dumbfounded at the audacity of the company. The company had become very desperate and aggressive and was trying to influence my decisions through Yui. Yui and I had stopped talking to each other except when the company wanted me to say yes to something they wanted.

10. A few days later, Mr. Kawasaki called me asking me to sign the contract. I curtly said 'no.'

11. About a week later I got a letter from Yui. [**Exhibit H1**][**Exhibit H2**]

Seems like the computer works people had already prepared the contract and wanted me to sign it and wanted my answer by Jan 7th, for some non-explainable reason. My objections to Yui were all in vain. When I reminded her that I was looking for finance jobs and not some computer jobs, she was calm and asked me about the problem. She said, "Just sign it and work for Mitsubishi Electric and if you don't like the job, search for another job." I had to say yes again and I remember the company taking 2-3 weeks to send the contract. I signed it and sent it to the company.

11. Mr. Urabe phoned at least one more time later informing Yui that they were setting up a comfortable work environment for me.

Comment: First Mr. Kobayashi from head office and later Mr. Urabe got in the habit of making frequent calls to Yui. When I came to Japan, Yui on two separate occasions told me that she and her mother were so proud of me for having been hired by Mitsubishi Electric.

12. In between, I got my green card, went for a few interviews, got interviewed by four companies in the same trip [**Exhibit I1**], got hired by Foster Higgins, world's largest actuarial firm and Independence Blue Cross. [**Exhibit I2**]. Morgan Stanley in New York called and told me they were very much interested in hiring me. (A few years later, I got a call from the office of Chief Actuary of Social Security Administration asking me they were very much interested in hiring me if I had US citizenship).

I had to decide what to do next.

Weighing the Options

By the time I was through with Mitsubishi Electric's recruitment process, I knew that I didn't want to continue with Yui. First, I thought of the job with them and wondered if it was in related to marrying her. If so, then I was out. At no time Mitsubishi raised this and I had to assume that it was not. Actually, I felt ashamed about prejudging them assuming if it was true they would have certainly told me this being such a major point related to employment.

Initially, I thought of moving and changing my phone number and not being bothered by Yui so that I could stay in the US and pursue my dreams. Finally, I decided that she deserved better and I had to go to Japan to break up with her.

Then I thought of Mitsubishi Electric. It was obvious that hiring me was very significant for them. They had a very bad reputation mistreating minorities and women. Perhaps they were trying to change. I thought they should have hired some Chinese for historical reasons but I could understand given their history, no Chinese or Korean wanted to work for them and so instead, they had settled on me. They had to start with someone.

They knew from my resume that I had a green card, was looking for the investment analyst career, and was much above-average in academic, and in spite of my repeated refusals went through Yui to force me to say yes. Going through a woman on their part showed me that they were desperate to hire me. Mitsubishi Electric was a total failure in computers and a person like me could do wonders for them. Was their recruitment to make me a star or was it to harass me was a question on my mind. I was going to be at their mercy in Japan.

I thought of the possibility of them having evil intentions but had to rule this out. And if by chance they tried something funny, I had my full armor with me and was like a porcupine. Permanent job status had its privilege and mainly it gave me the right to be treated like a Japanese and it also ensured support of their labor union (I was wrong here too. Their labor union generally supports the management.) I had an US green card, so I had a strong safety net. I could get support of Western media (shows how naive I was.) I came to the conclusion that even though I would be working in a very notorious company, they wouldn't dare to mistreat me because of the potential high price they would have to pay.

On the other hand, if they were rational, they would treat me very well. Mitsubishi group has not become a hugely successful group by taking hasty, irrational decisions and had to be admired for hiring a person of my caliber who can help them succeed in the coming century.

I was 32 years old which was a bit late for entry into financial fields and if I didn't join the industry then it would have been over for my intended career in the field that I wished to pursue. It was a now or never moment for my career. I thought about this and thought Mitsubishi Electric must have thought of that too.

But the condition about leaving them in 5 years as told by Mr. Kawasaki was bothering me. Why will they hire someone as a permanent employee only to tell him that he will have to leave after 5 years? I thought that if things went wrong, me being the first permanent employee of theirs, of course I didn't want to stick around and was open to leaving them on mutually agreeable terms getting compensating handsomely in the form of severance pay. There was a second possibility. One group of the company wanted to open its door and wanted to hire me, and there was another conservative group, which didn't want me. For the enlightened group to succeed, I had to stay there and fight the conservative group. I was ready for that.

I had asked to be the head of Mitsubishi's operation in India in 5 years and thought the company understood that it was a reasonable request. After the interview with Mr. Kawasaki, I didn't call them back and instead the company started the talks again. To me it meant that they had blinked and had agreed to my requests. Also, I had to assume that my talents were on par with the best in the company, and being a permanent employee, if I performed well, I had a decent shot at being their senior executive and even clinching the enviable position of CEO; very reasonable in my view. However, I had to be careful.

My future relationship with Emma was an issue of which I had to think of. I thought we were a good match, and our relationship was on some sort of hold because of my stress trying to get the green card and distance of hundreds of miles between us. After getting the green card, I would move to a different place making our relationship firmer. We talked a long time on phone [**Exhibit A2**]

a few days before I had to leave the USA. Finally, I decided I couldn't manage so many things and decided to focus on Mitsubishi Electric for pioneering thawing of racial inequality at Mitsubishi. I thought Mitsubishi thing was so huge for the human race!

My coming to Japan to work for Mitsubishi Electric was the start of my adventure into the unknown like that of Netaji Subhas Chandra Bose who had boarded the ill-fated Japanese plane several decades ago.

The Experiment

I arrived in Japan and was welcomed by Yui and her father who picked me up from the airport. Within a couple of hours of picking me up, she told me that she did not love me anymore and didn't want to marry me which led to a big relief on my part. I told her since I was in Japan because of her, we should continue and see what happened because I wanted to give her a chance but judging from her behavior and mental status I had no expectation that it will improve at all.

We went to the Mitsubishi Electric's computer works together and met with Mr. Sawai, the *bucho* – senior guy) and Mr. Ono, the *kacho*. After some small talk, Mr. Sawai asked me how long I planned to be with them. I remembered Mr. Kawasaki telling me that I will have to leave after 5 years and I had come to the conclusion that some bad elements in the company didn't want me and I thought that they were indeed those bad elements. I knew that in about 6 months, the head office will pull me there and since my stay with these bad elements was going to be short so why antagonize them by telling 'till retirement' or something like that. I smiled very broadly and told them 'I guess 5 years or so' which seemed to make them happy. I was happy knowing that in 6 months I will be in headquarters being groomed for something big. Well, that's what I thought then.

Mr. Sawai informed me that they didn't know where to place me and decided on the system architecture department because the general level of English was high there. They assigned me to work with Dr. Shinya Fushimi, to support SQL interface around his database engine - GREO. I said whatever remembering Mr. Kawasaki telling me that they had hired me for developing financial system but I was not in a mood to fight.

The computer works was in Ofuna. Yokohama and Kamakura, the old capital of Japan, were close by. The company-provided apartment was about a 5 minute walk from the computer works entrance.

Japanese Language Immersion

The very first thing which I noticed was there was no sign of any attempt to make my workplace convenient for me. Did they not get the memo? It puzzled me but considering that I would be in head office after 6 months, I didn't want to complain needlessly and stand out. There is a reason for everything.

Dr. Fushimi, a graduate of elite University of Tokyo, was a star performer. His GREO database machine had landed him a medal from the company's president. He had spent a year or two in the US at IBM's research lab and had very good English language abilities. He was very helpful and we used to talk often whenever he was in the section, since he spent a lot of time with the other teams.

I started working on SQL. About that time I was really curious about why was I recruited so aggressively. Obviously, it had nothing to do with SQL which was very simple! So one day after being in the company for 2-3 weeks, I asked Dr. Fushimi. He responded that he had looked at my resume, was impressed but didn't see anything on it which made about 16 executives sign the papers to hire me. He was surprised about my hiring. That put to rest my worries and I knew with so many having interest in me, good things were going to come my way and there was no need to be rattled by small matters. I thought it is just their inexperience and culture and things would sort out in due course. I just had to be patient.

Weekly group meetings were held in Japanese. In the beginning, somebody, likely Dr. Fushimi or Mr. Ono, gave a brief summary of events at the end for my benefit but later when he was not there or even when present briefs became really brief and later, vanished altogether.

A few weeks in the job, I was sent all alone to a remote computer system to do some testing for considerable time of couple of weeks or so - and everything was in Japanese, even the computer system and the manuals. I had to do everything by guesswork. It was a slow and frustrating experience.

Mr. Sawai used to test out my Japanese language skills in front of the team by telling me something in Japanese - and when I looked confused, I could see the team members' piercing and disapproving eyes.

Mr. Ono asked me to introduce Japanese language in my write ups. [**Exhibit J**]

I had earlier asked Mr. Ono about how to go about improving my Japanese, hoping some help might be provided. Instead he told me to buy a TV set, just like other Indians and Pakistanis do, which would help me in learning Japanese,. He was a graduate of Tokyo Institute of Technology, Japan top-ranked technical school, and was a simple man.

At the beginning, Mr. Takatani tried to help me a little by bringing a hiragana and katakana character listings. He also helped decipher some of the kanjis for me. But for the most part, I was on my own. When I asked him about the names of language schools, he shrugged his shoulders. After work, I was left on my own and in an alien country without any language skills; it was an ordeal to accomplish even small tasks.

The company was not going to provide me any help in Japanese language training because it would be 'unfair' to its Japanese employees but wanted me to master Japanese language as quickly as possible as was evident from their behavior. It seemed like the company had extremely high expectations of me concerning Japanese language learning and were expecting me to master both written and verbal Japanese almost instantly. Because of this extreme pressure, I was spending all my free time in language schools [**Exhibit K1**] and memorizing flash cards or reading books or listening to language tapes [**Exhibit K2**]. I spent a few thousand hours doing so. I could think of two reasons - one they didn't have experience with foreigners and didn't know that it took a lot of effort to learn the Japanese language, and second that they were testing me out to see how tough I was so that I would be groomed for better jobs in future.

Times became intolerable and I went to the Berlitz language school, a popular school in nearby Yokohama- they tested me – found that I didn't know any Japanese and I was placed at level F+ [Exhibit L1], and was suggested a training program [Exhibit L2]. It was quite expensive though and I couldn't pay from my pockets as I had done for all other schools and books. I brought it to the company's attention but it was ignored.

I also started wondering about my transfer to the head office. A couple of times Mr. Ono mentioned to take me to head office but they were just in passing and nothing came out of it.

One interesting thing that I observed a few months at the job was that my colleagues were going for company-sponsored English-language classes. That surprised me since the company had been telling me the Japanese staff didn't get any language training. There were English language proficiency tests that everyone, including me, had to take. [Exhibit M] My attention now was for the newly hired temporary workers scheduled to come in a few months. I wanted to see how they handled the language-barrier.

Job Performance

As Mr. Sawai had told me on the very first day, they didn't know where to put me and had decided on System Architecture Group because English level proficiency was high there and I was assigned to help Dr. Fushimi by dealing with SQL development. I had never dealt with SQL before that and it was a very simple language. Dr. Fushimi was rarely in the section, was at other sections with others but did come for the weekly meeting every Monday morning. He was a very professional and friendly person and answered any questions from me patiently.

He was apparently very pleased with my work and later when he was trying to solve a sub-query problem, an important step whose execution is very time consuming unless the query is flattened and no vendor we tested had provided flattening it to make it a quicker process (nowadays almost all provide that) he gave the assignment to me saying that I was very smart and only I could do it. It was flattering and motivating. At first, I was scared and wondered why I was given the task since in all likelihood I would fail in that task. About one month of hard work paid off, and I was able to come up with an algorithm to flatten the sub-queries and make execution time faster by order of magnitude. For example, instead of the 2 hours the original query took, the flattened version of it took just a few seconds for its execution.

Marriage Pressure

The company made sure everyone around me knew that I was going to marry a Japanese woman. The housing they provided was for married employees. Company's newsletter staff after interviewing me mentioned that I was going to marry a Japanese girl. The only trouble was that I was not told.

A few weeks in the job, Mr. Sawai started ordering me to marry my 'fiancée'. I politely told him that I was not sure which seemed to upset him. A few months later I casually remarked to Ms. Inoue, a colleague in my section that one of her friends who used to come and eat lunch in our section was attractive. Mr. Sawai ordered Ms. Inoue to ask her to go out with me. Ms. Inoue was horrified and remarked in our section that her friend already had a boyfriend and sensing trouble I stopped even looking at her.

Mr. Sawai also started asking me to vacate the apartment because it was meant for married employees. I had to remind him that it was in my contract.

A few weeks after her initial reaction of her not wanting to marry me, Yui had again started pressurizing me to marry her. When I told that I didn't love her, she wondered what had love got to do with marriage. Only later when I met Kaoru, a kind, understanding person who seemed God-sent at that difficult phase of my life, I was able to break up with Yui.

A Caucasian at Workplace

While I was struggling with intense pressure put on me to master Japanese language, about 6 months in the job Mr. Ono announced that he was going to the US with other executives to hire temporary workers. It made me happy because I expected them not to get any Japanese language training (because it would be unfair to Japanese workers) and see them struggle and then the company would definitely realize that learning Japanese language is difficult.

About one year since I joined the company, Mr. Bitar, the Caucasian foreigner born in Lebanon, arrived at the Computer works. Previously, he had been in the PhD program of prestigious Princeton University's computer science program but had dropped out after completing its master's level courses (many do so either because they lose their interest or they fail their preliminary exams. I think Mr. Bitar lost interest. He was very bright.) Mitsubishi Electric had gone to top schools in the US and UK like MIT, Caltech, UC-Berkeley. Mr. Ono was part of the team that went to USA, and managed to get one or two from these schools. All such new employees' were on a one year contract but that was extendable to 5 years (just like mine who was on permanent contract but could work for 5 years as Mr. Ono had explained to me). Before he came, arrangements were made for English-language software and manual.

He sat facing me in the team of about 7 or 8. I was looking for signs that he had had a hard time adjusting to Japanese-language environment like I had, but I failed to see that in him. Mr. Ono talked to him in Japanese. He smiled and nodded often, with words 'Hai' and 'wakarimashita'. It was remarkable - either he was really a genius or was he faking it? The faces of my colleagues were beyond description - they lightened up - and words like 'sugoi ne' (isn't it wonderful) were floating in the air until their heads turned towards me and their faces transformed to that of disdain. Finally, they couldn't hold their feelings back and started saying openly 'you are stupid' or something similar. I tried to argue with Mr. Suzuki that it was impossible for a foreigner not exposed to Chinese characters to master both the verbal and written Japanese in just one year, he replied he knew foreigners who had done so and when asked to show me just one of them, he didn't respond. [**Exhibit N**] shows my Japanese Level Proficiency Exam Level 1 results - in three years passing the highest level exam with scores good enough for top private schools like Keio and Waseda which is quite rare for a foreigner and full-time non-students not exposed to Chinese-characters earlier). Mr. Ono chimed in stating that I have been found to be incompetent in Japanese learning and the head office has mandated that I be transferred to the USA.

Anyway, back to Mr. Bitar. He was a friendly guy and I asked him how he learned such good Japanese. He replied Berlitz in the US where the company (Mitsubishi Electric) paid for his 100 lessons. He said initially their contract didn't have such good language learning clause but later the company had a change of heart and provided them with generous language training. Soon he, along with other newly arrived foreigners, was to attend Berlitz in Yokohama, where I had checked earlier. On top of that, he could study for a few hours at workplace. When I told him that the company didn't give me any training, he replied that I didn't know how to ask because they are very kind and nice and gave them training even without asking and much more than that were previously agreed to in their contracts. On another separate occasion, he mentioned that the HR people had told him how I got my job and smiled as if he had some insiders' knowledge.

At that time, I talked to Mr. Ono and he gave me permission to study Japanese for an hour each day. I started with my studies. Mr. Sawai, the *bucho* and boss of Mr. Ono, the *kacho*, used to go to his desk following a different route but very soon he started taking detour so that he could pass near my desk and was able to observe what books I was reading. After a week or so, he told me that when the Japanese staff went to USA, they were not allowed to study English at workplace. I quit studying at workplace and my search for a good lawyer intensified.

Search for Justice

I contacted the Foreigner Affairs Office in Yokohama but after some running around, I got the impression that the lady had talked to the company and was just giving me false assurances. I started looking for lawyers. I wrote to the Tokyo Bar Association and they forwarded it to Mr. Satoshi Murata who headed Human Rights for Foreigners Section and a meeting was arranged where I presented my case in very broken Japanese to a team of about a dozen or so lawyers. Mr. Murata wanted to take up the case and wrote a letter to the company as to why I was not given Japanese language training. Suddenly, the company sprang into action with me being taken to meetings where everything was recorded and I got the feeling they were trying to find out if I had a green card and they were instead trying to shift the blame on Mr. Ono, perhaps the most innocent one.

About the time the discontent was brewing, I was told that they have an Indian engineer in a permanent job in Nagoya and I should go and see him. Finally, one day he showed up, a graduate of IIT, Kharagpur and married to a Japanese woman. I thought that he looked a little like a Japanese person. He didn't seem happy with me, told me not to compare myself with the Caucasian colleagues who were special, and told me to ask the company for my needs. Mr. Sawai too told me that the company was willing to talk to me provided I didn't bring my lawyer. I was no match for their combined cunning, and thought any talk with them would not compensate adequately for the damage to my career and fighting them seemed like the only option I had.

Coverage

Mr. Satoshi Murata and Mr. Kondo, my lawyers, had arranged for a press conference and a small bite from that made it to the evening news of NHK, Japan's official TV station. Japan's biggest business newspaper, Nihon Keizai Shinbun, had couple of articles on it, favoring me. Nihon Kogaku, Japan's only law review monthly magazine published an interview with me. [**Exhibit O**] Some time ago, it had published an interview with Myanmar's popular human rights activist, Aung San Suu Kyi. It seemed to me that the Japanese media [**Exhibit P**] would have pursued it if the Indian news media were interested in it too. Unfortunately, this was not the case.

I talked to Mr. Pillai of Indian wire services and he would have nothing of it. He was just not interested in it. After a long conversation trying to persuade him, I gave up. My family found one line coverage like "Kamal Sinha, an Indian scientist, sues Mitsubishi Electric for discrimination" in the local Patna newspaper. Please don't bang your head in frustration if you missed that news.

American media was also not interested in it. The New York Times reporter was friendly but told me they covered the story only in case of Chinese employees with PhDs. I didn't know if he was just joking. Business week seemed interested and wanted to interview me but at the very last moment sent me an official letter cancelling it.

The Western reporter from India Abroad weekly based in the USA called me and talked at length with me and published it.

After the lawsuit

About a week into the lawsuit apparently, my apartment owned by Mitsubishi Electric was bugged. I tried to make phone calls, and the strong static would start in about 5-10 seconds making conversation all but impossible. I complained to KDD, the phone company about this strong static but the complaint was shrugged off. I continued to live with it. About a year later, I read an article in Japan Times about how some companies were wire-tapping their employees' phone lines and the number one symptom of it was strong static. This time I checked outside my apartment and I saw a line going into a small switchboard. This time, I went to KDD and informed them that my line is bugged and if they don't do something about it, I will have to go to the police. The static stopped after a day or so. I checked and there was no sign of that wire and the switchboard. As if it was just a figment of my imagination.

I used to walk in the evenings and often went to *daibutsu* (Big Buddha) statue in Kamakura, not far from my apartment. After meeting Mr. Morimoto, head of personnel department, I knew it was not fair but his face looked like he could murder somebody. I was scared for my life. Through Kaoru, whose father knew a few top lawyers, I met one of them and he told me that I was irritating to Mitsubishi Electric like a mosquito but I hadn't reached the level that they will feel the need to eliminate me. That assured me somewhat and once in my life I was happy to be like a mosquito.

My lawyers told me that I will have to remain with the company while the lawsuit was progressing. The lawsuit progress was extremely slow – I remember after one court session, the next one was after 9 months or so. After a total of nearly 6 years of frustration, I had had enough and decided to come back to the US in 1995. The lawsuit continued.

At the job, people stopped talking to me and I was given some useless work. I could not concentrate at all. The cleaning lady was nice to me and one Japanese engineer came to me one day and told me what the company did to me was very unfair. There might have been a few others like him but nobody else dared talk to me. They were hired for life and most planned to remain there for a very long time possibly until retirement and a simple reckless behavior like talking to me or smiling at me would have doomed their entire future career.

I also heard from a Japanese lawyer that the company was engaged in a legal battle with a Japanese staff. If I remember correctly, it had been going on for years, more than twenty years or so. I think his issue was about the workers' right to have another labor union. During the time he was fighting the company, likely he didn't get any raises and his salary would have been half or less of that of others who joined the company with him. And since he was Japanese, foreign or even domestic media was not interested in covering his story.

Mr. Bitar, and another Caucasian who used to be seen around, were not affected by my lawsuit at all or were not interested. Life was good for him as it is for most Caucasians in Japan.

Repercussions

As to be expected, this experience had lots of adverse effects on me. During Mitsubishi Electric days because of all the stress and poor diet (there was no food at Mitsubishi Electric for vegetarians) [**Exhibit Q**] I became obese with BMI over 30 (about 20 kilogram overweight) . Later, I lost weight through a lot of hard work and now am of normal weight but the ill effects lingered on. Later in the US, a cardiologist informed me that in the past (probably during those days) I had severe diabetes and as a result my arteries got messed up. There are probably some other serious side-effects from this experience such as very high blood pressure and some more issues that I am not aware of. While I seem reasonably healthy now, there is no telling what the future will bring on me and that is partly the reason I have decided to tell my story now before I become incapable of doing so.

Aptitude and Academics

(Note: Readers may skip this chapter.)

Keeping up with Indian tradition, I would have preferred to be very humble, and let someone else blow my horns. I felt it was not going to happen. At IIT, many told me that I was stupid with numbers and at Mitsubishi Electric many told me that I was stupid with languages. I wish to humbly state that they were all wrong.

Aptitude Test Scores

Verbal Aptitude

Since my verbal aptitude scores were the main reason Mitsubishi Electric decided to hire me, I think it requires some detailed description. I considered quantitative skills to be my forte and my verbal skills to be a distant second but during high school I had excellent command over Hindi language (reading and grammar) too. My command over English was poor and I was content to be just good enough to pass the board and entrance exams like the JEE. At IITB, I didn't consider the need to improve my English language proficiency until one day - I think it was during my third year when I was about 18 years -, I got hold of a sample GRE practice set from a classmate who was preparing to apply for US universities, and decided to test myself in the privacy of my hostel room. The experience was sobering - I scored in the first percentile in verbal section - obviously not the top but the bottom! I knew I was bad but such pathetic scores were beyond my imagination. Humbled, I decided to improve upon my English language skills. I worked on my vocabulary by practicing from those ubiquitous vocabulary builder books, and improved my reading comprehension by reading English novels and more importantly by reading books on improving reading comprehension. Those books were not easy to find and were expensive. The British Council library in Chennai was a great help in this regard. (And they kept their temperatures cool!) Within 7-8 years, I had scored 99% on the verbal section of GMAT exam. [**Exhibit R**] About that time, I managed to score a 98% on GRE verbal. I have heard of and met a few at the IIT who studied in prestigious English-medium private schools and thought in English rather than in their native languages, were expected to join IIMA or Stanford later, and no one would have been surprised if they announced that they obtained 99% on GMAT verbal section. It was expected but me? Ha ha ha. Let me use this moment to state my thoughts on that 99% achievement.

Achieving 99% is a noteworthy milestone but it really is a low bar. Really! About 2000 GMAT test takers each year had a score in that range during that period. Over a period of say 25 years, we are dealing with 500,000. Ignoring standard error issues that will magnify this number, 500,000 is a pretty large number. Assume if somebody informed Virat Kohli that he is in the top 500,000 cricket players, do you think he will be pleased?

Certain segments of IIT made it into a hyper competitive place. They liked bragging rights like "I was a straight A student," "I scored 99%+," I scored perfect 800 on the quant section." If they got anything lower, some of them repeated the test, not minding to pay over Rs 10,000 in current prices for the test fee. Given the uncertainties concerning the test taking process, small differences in test scores are considered equivalent by most schools, and it is pointless to repeat the test if someone already has near-perfect scores. But try to explaining that to the hyper competitive · crowd at IIT!

But coming back to my verbal scores; I believe broken down by component scores, I would have probably scored A+ in reading comprehension, A- in vocabulary, B in grammar, and C+ in my writing skills. All of them merged to give me a 98 or 99% score. So you can see that I am not a fan of these scores. However, 99% has a halo effect. And I used it and put it down on my resume.

Over time, I have realized that beginning from childhood, a foreign language can be mastered by quite a few, starting from young adulthood at age 18, to scoring a 99% in it 7-8 years later is a feat not many can claim because foreign language learning becomes more and more difficult as one grows older. I don't believe that many people can achieve what I was able to accomplish. Unfortunately, this caught the eye of Mitsubishi Electric.

During my second year at IIT, I took a course titled 'Introduction to Ethics' and it was taught by a professor from Oxford University, who was on a sabbatical at IITB.

When the results of the first mid-term were declared, many were devastated to learn that he had assigned zeros to their effort. To add salt on their wounds, they came to know that I had scored a perfect 10. Many came to me, asking for a look at my paper, and left looking confused. I too was unable to understand why I managed a perfect score. I attributed that to idiosyncratic nature of geniuses like the Oxford professor.

In 2013, about 20 of my batch mates from Hostel 7 had a reunion. I chanced upon a batch mate K., who had studied at a private English-medium school and had impeccable English skills (and yes he studied at IIMA).

He remarked, 'Kamal, you were judged on your content in that paper and obviously not the language.'

Oh, thanks! That happened about 40 years ago and he remembered that incident that I had nearly forgotten. I wanted to tell him about my 99% score but refrained.

Quantitative Aptitude

My career aspirations were driven by my high, extremely well, high quantitative aptitude. I made it to IITB and was in its selective electrical engineering section which makes it very obvious to many readers that I was blessed with very high quantitative aptitude. Duh will be the response of many. Based on my experience with aptitude tests and comments from others in the US, I think my skills were indeed special. Scoring just a plain vanilla 99% on quantitative aptitude tests would have been quite insulting for me. Instead, I always tried to get perfect scores and was disappointed when I made a few careless mistakes to lose a few points. For example in GMAT, I missed 4 questions out of 60 scoring a converted 56 [**Exhibit R**] - all because of careless mistakes which was frustrating- but it was still high enough so that if I omitted answering 10 questions on top of my 4 careless mistakes, I would have still scored 99%. And completing 30 minutes quantitative sections of GMAT in less than 11 minutes for me was normal for me completing them in leisurely pace. When I took the CAT exam for IIM 1981 entrance, I recall one quantitative section had 60 questions and we had just 10 minutes to complete that section. Questions were easy but will I have enough time to read the questions, let along answer all of them was the question in my mind and I did go fast. I completed that section in time. I guess I scored 50+. My guess is that the typical student accepted at the IIM's that year scored below 25, more likely around 10 to 15 in that section. Curiously, I got interview calls from Ahmedabad and Bangalore but not from Calcutta, which is supposed to be a quant school.

My quant professors in the US recognized my skills, and one of them, my operations research professor Dr. Marvin Troutt, who was an actuary too, encouraged me to become one since it involved high quantitative skills. That's what I was preparing for besides improving my investment and financial skills by passing CFA and CFP exams.

Other Aptitude Scores

Following have no direct bearing on my Mitsubishi Electric hiring or career aspirations but for the sake of completeness I will mention them. I scored 98% on analytical reasoning section of GRE. In spatial reasoning test when applying for Larsen & Toubro, the clerk who had graded the test, commented favorably on my performance.

Academic Performance

I was good in studies in high school thanks to excellent dedicated teachers like Mr. Nandi and Mr. Paul, I didn't study much during IIT days and studied very hard during my graduate days while pursuing first MBA and then MS in computer science at Southern Illinois University at Carbondale. In spite of my poor performance at IIT, after just one semester in my MBA program I was also able to secure admission at PhD program at prestigious University of Illinois, Urbana-Champaign's business school with scholarship [**Exhibit S1**] It was ranked #6 in the US. I remember the professor from Urbana telling me that they had not seen reference letters like the ones for me before.

My entrance to the MS computer science course makes for an interesting anecdote. My roommate, a graduate of IIT, Roorkee, was disdainful of MBA's and challenged me to take computer science course- IBM Assembly Language Programming which he found to be very challenging and which was considered to be one of the toughest pro-gramming courses offered in the program. I decided to take it during the summer session, when courses were paced at roughly twice the speed of regular Fall or Spring semesters and most students took only this course to do justice to it. I decided to register for 3 more courses after much argument with the Dean. The school didn't allow me to overload to 4 courses and I decided to take this course by not registering but attending the classes and the professor gracefully agreed to grade my tests and assignments. I scored the highest score in the course out of about 30 students. I also did well in the other 3 courses too. [**Exhibit S2**] Later, I de-cided to continue with computer science

Afterwards, I decided to conduct an experiment - to take the GRE Advanced Test in Computer Science at the start of my CS program, and then taking it again towards the end. This way, any improvement in my score could be attributed to the CS program, and my goal was to show that the program can compete with brand names like Stan-ford and MIT and learning depends mainly upon the stu-dent. When I took the GRE Advanced test within a few weeks in the program, about half the 80 questions covered material which I was not exposed to. I answered the rest. I scored 750 which placed me in the 91th percentile. Earlier I had obtained admission material from PhD in Computer Science program at Stanford, which was and still is one of the best programs in the world, and it showed background of its incoming PhD students - most had completed MS in computer science which was not surprising but the surpris-ing part was it mentioned median advanced test score of its incoming PhD students and it was 750 – exactly the same as mine. It actually discouraged me from taking the follow up advanced test towards the end of the program realizing that I didn't have much to improve on. What a pity!

Later I studied for certification in Actuarial Science by taking Society of Actuaries exams. I was working at the University of Tennessee at Martin at that time and during my free time, studied for them. They were very challenging and most actuaries who worked in the industry got free time, study material, exam fees, training reimbursement, promotion etc. I had no such benefits. I went faster than most, and scored quite high all in my first attempts [**Exhibit T**] even though I sweated through some of them thinking the actuaries who set the questions on those tests were sadists. When I went for interviews, potential employers seemed to be impressed. To make up for lost time, I decided to go faster by getting my CFA and CFP certifications too [**Exhibit U**]. CFA had lots of reading material for each level exam (over 1000 pages each) but I thought it was an easy track but investor bankers proudly displaying the CFA designation after their name might disagree vigorously. The level 1 covered economics and I thought I did very well (almost perfect - among the highest perhaps) in that section (they don't disclose the scores though). CFP was tougher, I scored on average 95% on 6 exams, and I wouldn't be surprised if very few people, if any, exceeded that. I took all three concurrently and added to the challenge which motivated me.

Afterword

One interesting thing happened when I started fighting my legal battle against Mitsubishi Electric in Japan. At the beginning, I didn't let my attorneys know my true thoughts about why the company behaved the way it did because I thought that if I tell them that I was just being used as a guinea-pig in their experiment, they would not take my case thinking that I was all bonkers and delusional. In the Tokyo court, it was filed as a simple case of discrimination – the Japanese staff had received English-language training while I didn't get any Japanese-language training. What surprised me was that after a few sessions of legal arguments in the court with almost no feedback from me, from my limited understanding of their legal briefs written in Japanese language, I realized that they had understood what really happened. They were very intelligent – graduates of Keio and Waseda, Japan's top two private universities, and had passed their bar exams which had the passing rate of 2% in the hyper competitive Japanese education system. In my view that was not the main reason. I think there were three main reasons – 1) they were aware of how lowly a Mitsubishi Electric company can behave when dealing with a non-Caucasian foreign worker 2) they were open to evidence and came to conclusion only after weighing it, and 3) they believed in me.

I will contrast their behavior with that of Indians whom I tried telling about my experience. Among many, they included a a PhD from MIT, Cambridge, batch mates from IIT among them one who received a PhD From UC, Berkeley, and one who had done very well at IIM, Ahmedabad. Obviously they were no intellectual slouches and would be considered among the elites who India is counting on to usher itself into superpower status. Their behavior was very consistent. Nobody was interested in what I had to say about my experience. Just a few words like 'I worked at Mitsubishi Electric in Japan. They harassed me.' was generally good enough for getting a strong reaction from some of them. Calling me a liar or something similar and reluctant to hear any more words from me was their reaction. When I tried to warn the dean of recruitment at IITB about Mitsubishi, it appeared that he was an admirer of Mitsubishi companies and was not open to hearing what I had to say. Email to the Director went unanswered.

I have a feeling that if I had tried to get a reaction out of the elites of India simply using choice-words for their parents or their abilities they are so proud of, it simply wouldn't cut it. They were well above it. However, if I used words to tell facts like "Mitsubishi Electric harassed me," "Many whites are racists" their bodies would start trembling uncontrollably and vigorously with anger, as it contradicts hundreds of years of their genetic and environmental makeup, and while they are bovine in almost all their behavior, for once, in order to defend their masters' reputation, they might turn more vicious than even the most dreaded ISIS..

As long as people like them remain in power, I don't see any future for India. It's only a new breed of leaders, free of deep-rooted slave genes, who can take India to a glorious future.

The US Experience

This book is about my experience in Japan. I came back to the US after that. I will write about my American experience later but wanted to recount one typical event from there. Consider this to be a gentle preview of American life.

It was during my graduate days in computer science. Academically, I was doing well. I aced all the classes except maybe one or two where I managed a second position. I was very motivated and was studying real hard. One day Dr. Varol, who was in charge of financial aid, smiled at me and congratulated me on he having been asked by Dr. Robert (Bob) McNeil to assign me to him as his graduate assistant the coming semester. I was happy after hearing about this apparent honor until another Indian teaching assistant on hearing this news from me told me to be careful because Bob had a reputation of being a 'redneck.' I didn't know what that term exactly meant but knew that it was derogatory. I didn't feel apprehensive though and thought it was another chance to impress another professor. However, a few months ago an Indian British student had told me that he was suspended by Bob for a semester for cheating allegation and he had to go to the university senate to overturn Bob's decision. He was obviously very upset and had very low opinion about Bob. I listened to him but was not convinced of his innocence. I thought he got off because of a lack of conclusive evidence otherwise Bob must have had some strong reason to take such a drastic action.

Well, initial days working for Bob were uneventful. He asked me to write solutions to computer lab assignment which I did very willingly because it gave me a chance to show off my programming skills and it hardly took any time. I had to grade the lab solutions and tests. There were two mid-term exams and for the first one he gave Linda (the other TA) and me, copies of the exam to solve in advance to make sure nothing was wrong or ambiguous in the test paper. So far; so good.

He had to be out of town during the mid-term 1. He asked me to proctor that exam and announced this in the class a few times. The exam center was a fairly large hall with capacity of about 300 with many doors on both sides and towards the back. I distributed 92 papers. I noticed an Indian girl among the students. I collected the papers after one hour and later counted only 91 papers. One paper was missing. Promptly I informed Bob when he came back.

Within a few days his attitude towards me became very hostile and insulting. Even Linda noticed it and asked me what was the matter with Bob and why was he being so mean to me. I obviously assumed that it was related to the missing test paper. I thought that some student who did extremely badly on the test in disgust took his paper with him. It didn't make complete sense but that's what I could think of that time. I didn't know not collecting a paper was such a serious matter especially I couldn't have managed the students in such a big hall. I told him that in future we should allow the student to exit through one door only, an idea he rejected right away. His behavior was such and the way he looked at me that I started thinking he was mentally unstable.

In one meeting, he lifted his hand towards me and I really thought he was going to hit me. I ducked him which infuriated him and asked me why I did so. I kept quite not wanting to deal with a mad white professor. You don't want to mess with a white guy, mad or otherwise, if I had to summarize my experience in the USA.

For the next test only Linda was given the questions in advance.

It all disturbed me a lot and I stopped studying. Towards the end of the semester, I asked one student in the class who came to see me in the office what was the matter with Bob. She told me that there was an Indian female student in the class, who had done very poorly under Bob in a previous course, had scored almost a perfect score in midterm 1. And he suspected me. She added that this girl, apparently from Hong Kong, had a Chinese boyfriend who was a very good student and who was not enrolled in the class. Mystery of the missing test paper was clear to me. I think all students in the class knew what had happened except for Bob.

He also found mistakes with my solutions to the programming assignments and told the students that I didn't know how to code. I thought he was trying to take it on me for fooling him, as he thought, by helping that below-average Indian female student. I decided to tell Dr. Varol about it and went to him. I had taken three courses under him and had scored the highest in all of them. He told me that Bob found my solutions lacking in quality and he (Dr. Varol) was not willing to talk any further on that topic.

I thought Bob was particularly mean and was the Judge, Jury and Jerk in this matter but after dealing with many Americans, mostly whites, and many Chinese, and some browns like the Indians, over a long time in America, I have come to conclusion that Bob was just a normal American, nothing more, nothing less.

Exhibits

Exhibit A1 (top): Emma's introduction letter.

Exhibit A2 (bottom): Phone calls to Emma before leaving.

Exhibit B: Yui's letter urging me to come to Japan.

Exhibit C: Green Card petition approval

Exhibit D: My resume

Exhibit E1: Yui's letter regarding Mitsubishi's interest

Exhibit E2: Yui's letter from Exhibit E1 continued.

Exhibit F: Mitsubishi's job ad for system engineers

Exhibit G: Application form filled by Yui. 'fiancée'

Exhibit H1: Letter from Yui, contract is ready

Exhibit H2: Exhibit H1 continued.

Exhibit I1: Interview schedule with 4 actuarial firms

Exhibit I2: Job offer from Foster Higgins

Exhibit J: My weekly reports written in Japanese

Exhibit K1: Attending a language school in Sinjuku

Exhibit K2: Partial list of books and tapes

Exhibit L1: Berlitz's F+ evaluation of my Japanese skills

Exhibit L2: Berlitz's cost estimates

Exhibit M: My English language evaluation by Mitsubishi

Exhibit N: Japanese proficiency test results after 3 years

Exhibit O: Nihon Hougaku interview

Exhibit P: Press coverage of my lawsuit

Exhibit Q: Non-vegetarian lunch menu

Exhibit R: GMAT verbal score

Exhibit S1: Admission letter from Urbana-Champaign

Exhibit S2: 3 plus one unlisted course during summer

Exhibit T: Actuarial exam results

Exhibit U: CFA and CFP results

9/29/87

Dear TN-WHD-M,

I thought I would write
to let you know that I
liked your profile & that you

Let me introduce myself.
My name is
Kara ——————, & I live in
Winston-Salem, NC. I joined
Vege-Dates about 2 months ago

Exhibit A1 (top): Emma's introductory letter.

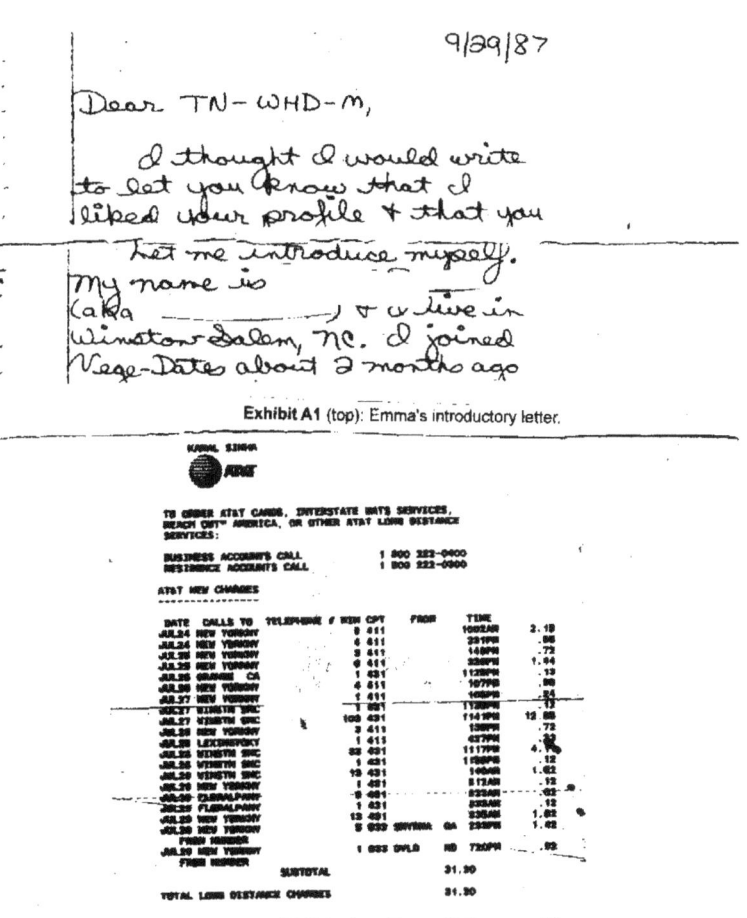

Exhibit A2 (bottom): Phone calls to Emma just prior to leaving the US.

Exhibits A1 and A2

June 24

Kamal—

I know we quarrel every time we talk
on the phone. It must be one of the reasons that
I miss you and I do want you to leave the States
for me alone soon. I know how you've been
worried about your Visa waiting for a long
time since I've been waiting for you, just
believing we can get together someday. This
two years were very long for my age and
still I feel uneasy about our future.

"Can't you leave the States for a few weeks
before you finally have an interview with the
Immigration people? Do you have to always
stay in your house before the interview?
If you can visit us just for a short,
you'd be able to see many things about Japan,
and you can decide what to do. Otherwise
I won't see you for a while. But I hope it
won't be more than 6 months. (Actually I didn't
understand why you mentioned 6 months this time)

This morning when I woke up, I thought it's
all over between us and cried. You're
always angry with me and me with you, too.
I wish we can be all right soon.
This letter may make you angry and
irritated. But it's all about what I want
to let you know. I don't mind putting
up with any hard time if we are together.
Would you think of our present happiness,

Exhibit B: Yui's letter dated June 24, 1988 urging me to come to Japan.

Exhibit B

64

6-6-88

Immigration and Naturalization Service

425 Eye Street N. W.
Washington, D.C. 20536

FILE: Memphis (SRC)

IN RE: Petitioner: The University of Tennessee at Martin
        Beneficiary: Kamal SINHA

PETITION: Petition to Classify Preference Status of Alien on Basis of
            Profession Pursuant to Section 203(a)(3) of the Immigration and
            Nationality Act, 8 U.S.C. 1153(a)(3)

IN BEHALF OF PETITIONER: R.W. Foley
                              2345 Cheshire Bridge Road
                              Atlanta, Georgia 30324

DISCUSSION: The third preference visa petition case was denied by the
director, Southern Regional Service Center, and a subsequent appeal was
dismissed. The matter is now before the Commissioner on motion to
reconsider. The motion will be granted and the appeal will be sustained.

Accordingly, eligibility has now been established. The beneficiary has the
requisite educational requirement to satisfactorily perform the job. The
order dismissing the appeal will be withdrawn, and the petition will be
approved.

ORDER: The order of October 27, 1987 is withdrawn. The petition is
            approved.

DATED: 27 MAY 1988   FOR THE ASSOCIATE COMMISSIONER
                                       EXAMINATIONS

                                       Thomas W. Simmons, Chief
                                       Administrative Appeals Unit

Exhibit C: Green Card petition approval by USCIS, Administrative Board of Appeals, Washington DC

Exhibit C

65

RAHUL SINHA

E-13 University Courts, Martin, TN 38237 . (901) 587-6593

OBJECTIVE

INVESTMENT ANALYST - where strong quantitative skills and ability to analyze financial data, evaluate modern technologies and research market conditions would be assets.

EDUCATION

M.S., Computer Science, Southern Illinois University, 1983-84. Normally completed all courses in the top 5%. High score (91%) on the GRE computer science test after brief exposure. Graduate assistant. According to my statistics professor: "One of the best five students I have ever taught."

M.B.A., Southern Illinois University, 1981-82. Graduate fellow - only 2 selected each year. High GMAT scores (quantitative : 56(99%), verbal : 47(99%)). Elected to Beta Gamma Sigma Honor Society. Completed 2 years' program in 16 months. Dr. Troutt, my operations research professor, whom I assisted in research and teaching, observed, "He is far and away the most able student I have encountered in our MBA, DBA programs."

B.Tech., Electrical Engineering, Indian Institute of Technology, 1973-78. Concentrated in semiconductor devices and telecommunications.

EXPERIENCE

ASSISTANT PROFESSOR - Taught computer programming and systems design courses. Instilled a love of computers in many students. (University of Tennessee at Martin, Sep. 1984 - May 1989)

SALES ENGINEER - In-charge of market research and new products. Conducted field trial of a new industrial product. Installed it under severe operating conditions at major customers' plants. Monitored its performance and sent reports to the R & D department. Result: Introduction of a very reliable product which soon became #1 selling product contributing about 15% to the division's revenue. (Larsen and Toubro Ltd., 1978-81)

PERSONAL DATA

Permanent resident. Born 1957. Excellent health. Enjoy reading, travel. Adept in Hindi. Some ability in Japanese language. Have passed the following exams: SOA's 100, 110, 120, 130, 140 and 151(average grade: 9+); CFA Level I ; CFP I,II,III,IV and V(average: 90%+)

PRIMARY AIMS AND ASSETS

Like to complete new tasks successfully and learn new things . . . Enjoy challenges . . . Believe that applying constructive imagination and perseverance are the keys to success.

Exhibit D: My resume.

Exhibit D

I.

July 16, '88

Hi Kamal,

Thanks for a birthday card for me. I hate I'm so old! I came back home yesterday from our school camping. On the second day we walked 20 kms and got tired so much. But everything went so good and anyway we enjoyed our trip.

About a week ago, there was a nice job ad. in the Japanese paper. I thought it very attractive, but at the same time, I thought it in vain to apply for the position for you. But my father found the ad and suggested that it must be a nice job for you. So anyway I decided to send your resume back in English and Japanese to them. I mailed them just before our school trip. Yesterday a personnel manager called so I wasn't home yet and my mother talked with him for a minute. She thought he might say they're not interested in you. But she was wrong. He said this company is really eager to let you work for them. So I called him back because I was asked to. We talked about you a little bit and he said that I should contact with you soon and ask if you're

Exhibit E1: Yui's letter dated July 16, 1988 regarding Mitsubishi Electric's interest in hiring me

Exhibit E1

67

interested in knowing more about their
company and talking about business things
recently. He said to get a working Visa
from Japanese administration is not easy and
that you really have to give evidence of working
in a certain company in Japan. And he
suggested that you can talk with the certain
people in U.S. office to help
you to decide to try this job or not.
The person I talked with on the phone sounded
very nice and generous and they're going to
set a comfortable circumstances for you, he said.
There are many foreign workers in the company
but not many in Computer laboratory
So if you're interested in this job, please
let me know. I have to call him back anyway
The company is Mitsubishi Electric Co.
capitalized at 1 billion dollars and one of the
leading electric companies Of course it's a member
of Mitsubishi group. I guess they want you
as one of the brains in their computer engineering
department, and I do want you to get contact
with them. My mother feels proud of you, too now.
Ma, too. Call me soon.
                                    Love,

Exhibit E2: Yui's letter from Exhibit E1 continued.

Exhibit E2

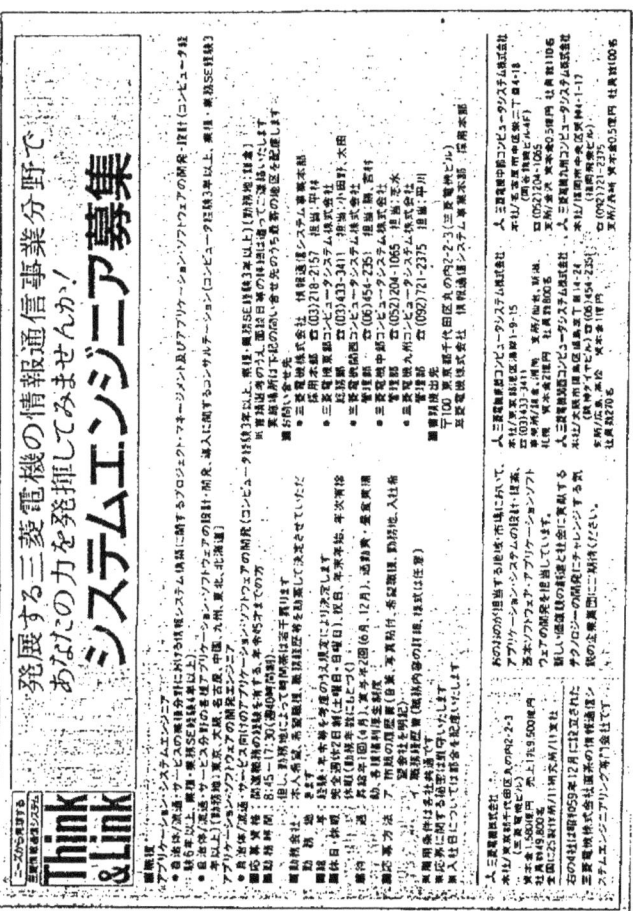

Exhibit F: Mitsubishi Electric's job ad regarding 'system engineers'.

Exhibit F

年	月	免許・資格

得意な学科		健康状態
		良好
趣味		志望の動機
旅行　読書		・挑戦 と 実力発揮
スポーツ		・結婚後 日本定住予定のため、自分の
バドミントン		専門分野が十分生かせる職に就き
		たい

本人希望記入欄(特に給料・職種・勤務時間・勤務地・その他についての希望などがあれば記入)
アプリケーション・システムエンジニア　東京勤務希望
三菱電機東部コンピュータシステム株式会社 入社希望

扶養家族名	性別	年令	扶養家族名	性別	年令

通勤時間　約　1時間　30分	扶養家族数(配偶者を除く)　　人	配偶者　有・無	配偶者の扶養義務　有・無

保護者(本人が未成年者の場合のみ記入)		電話
ふりがな		市外局番(　)
氏 名	住所〒(　 - 　)	(　)

コクヨ

Exhibit G: Application form filled by Yui. 'fiancée' and 'after marriage plans to live in Japan'

Exhibit G

70

Dec. 30

Kamal,

How are you?

I talked with Mr. Urabe who is in charge of dealing with your matter and I'm going to pick up some main points of the conditions written in a contract paper. He is now translating it into English so that you can understand it.

1. You'll be hired as a lifetime employee. (It's the first case with foreign workers, he said.) and you can work until 60.

2. Work for 8 hours a day and 2 days off a week. But sometimes you'll have to work longer or even on a holiday (you'll be paid for extra work).

3. monthly payment was 235,500 yen in 1988 and if you had worked in 1988, you could have got a bonus of 660,550 yen in December and another in June. It means you get about 4 million yen for a year without any over-time work.

4. Have to pay income tax, local tax.

Exhibit H1: December 1988 letter from Yui, Mitsubishi Electric had prepared the contract.

Exhibit H1

71

5. Have to pay insurance premium (Health, retiring ~~allowance~~ pension insurance etc.)

6. Company's apartment house rental 17,000 yen

7. You must become a member of Mitsubishi workers Union when you're hired.

? Mitsubishi will afford
   - your flight ticket (economy class) USA to Japan
   - transportation fare in Japan (Narita to Kamakura)
   - package of your things by air or by ship
     (less amount of 300,000 yen)
   ↳ you'll have to keep these receipt

What do you think of them ? Your work is to develop information - Processing systems. Or you can decide after you get here. ~~~~~ I must tell Mr. Urabe if you agree with these conditions generally or not by January 7, so please let me know. I tell you Mr. Urabe is very handsome & nice !

Write you.

Exhibit H2: Exhibit H1 continued.

Exhibit H2

72

JACOBSON ASSOCIATES
A DIVISION OF J.J.AH., LTD.

150 N. WACKER DRIVE
CHICAGO, ILLINOIS 60606
(312) 726-1578

Date: June 15, 1989

To: Kamal Sinha

From: Patty Jacobsen, Jacobson Associates

Subject: Itinerary for Interviews

You will be receiving your tickets from the travel agency.

* Sunday, June 18
  - arrive into Philadelphia, take a cab to the Latham Hotel,
    135 South 17th Street.

* Monday, June 19 (Interview with ▨▨▨▨▨▨▨▨▨▨▨▨)
  9:00 a.m.
  - Check out of hotel. Take a taxi to The Widener
    Building, 1339 Chestnut.
  - Go to the 9th floor (Human Resources), ask for
    Shelley Harris.
  - After the interview, take the Amtrak to the Princeton
    Junction. Upon arriving take a cab to the Office Park
    Hyatt. When you check in ask for the Bell Hop and tell
    him you'll need transportation to 212 Carnegie Center in
    the morning.

* Tuesday, June 20 (Interview with ▨▨▨▨▨▨▨▨)
  9:00 a.m.
  - Go directly to 2nd floor, ask for Kathy Moore.
  - Take all your luggage with you to the interview; they'll
    have a place for you to store your things.
  - When your interview is over, someone will take you to
    the train. Then you will go back to the Latham Hotel --
    you will be staying there for the duration.

* Wednesday, June 21 (Interview with ▨▨▨▨)
  9:00 a.m.
  - Take a cab to 1500 Market Square, 31st Floor.
  - Ask for Beverly Wilson.

* Thursday, June 22 (Interview with ▨▨▨▨▨▨▨▨▨▨▨▨
  ▨▨▨▨▨▨)
  9:00 a.m.
  - Take a train to New Brunswick.
  - Take a cab to 242 Old Brunswick Road, Suite 302.
  - Ask for Beverly Landstrom.

If you run into any problems, please call me. Good luck, Kamal!
Knock-em dead!

ATLANTA, GA ▪ CHICAGO, IL ▪ PHILADELPHIA, PA

Exhibit I1: My interview schedule with 4 actuarial firms in the USA all within a week.

Exhibit I1

73

Towers Perrin:
Greater Than The Sum Of Its Parts

You know us as *Cresap* — the firm to call when you need to improve your strategy and organizational effectiveness.

You know us as *Tillinghast* — the leading actuarial consultant to the insurance industry and provider of risk management consulting services to all industries.

You know us as *TPF&C* — the largest independent consulting firm providing total compensation, employee benefit, actuarial, communication and other human resource consulting services.

Now get to know us as *Towers Perrin* — the firm whose problem solving power reaches a new order of magnitude.

Towers Perrin

Mr. Kamal Sinha
June 28, 1989
Page 3.

convenience and ours, please bring them with you on your first day of employment. Please report to the Philadelphia Administrative Services Department, 26th floor, shortly before 9 a.m. to participate in the New Hires Orientation Program.

If you have any questions concerning the content of this letter or our earlier discussions, please don't hesitate to give me a call. I would like you to know that we all look forward to your joining Towers Perrin and the opportunity to work with you.

Sincerely,

Exhibit 12: Job offer from Foster Higgins, the largest actuarial firm in the world.

Exhibit 12

74

機方式グループ担当者週報	日時	平成2年11月29日
	報告者	ソンバ カワレ

今月の目標

SQL の書式照合せ

項目	今週の作業	来週の作業
1. SQL の書式照合せ	書式照合せのコンパイラーを開発には理論を読まなくてはならないと思って、始めにウルマン(Ullman)の本を読んでますがいいのですが、これを通して一通りよくど、ほかのつ、たとえばUNIX環境とYACCの勉強も出来るつもりです。	コンパイラーの本を読えることでみ
2. 日本語のSQLの本	トニューに読んでみましょうまず	始こせこせまみ

項目	今週の作業	来週の作業
1. YACCコンパイラー	YACCの作者のジョンソンさんの記事を読んでいます。	UNIXの環境やYACCに慣れるよりに、小さなプログラムをコンピューターに入れて、実行するつもりです。→同じように続けると思います。
2. ウルマンの本	ゆっくりコンパイラーの理論を勉強しています。	
3. 日本のSQL	この資は少しむしが出て調へませんでした。「時間がないから」	

作業上の問題点

OS/2の上で作ったプログラムを別々のページに印刷するために、先週の土理、ずっとTRYしましたが、プリンターのdefault line count は ページの line count と違うみたいでした。それで、たれか OS/2 をよく知っている人に教えてもらよりにお聞きしたいのですが...

竹谷さんに協力頼みました。
I had asked to Mr Takatani' support you on this problem.

Exhibit J: Two weekly reports written in Japanese language. Shows reports of December 1990.

Exhibit J

75

 **INTERNATIONAL EDUCATION CENTER**
21 Yotsuya 1-chome, Shinjuku-ku,
Tokyo 160 Japan
Phone:(03)359-9621~8

To : Mr. / Ms. _SINHA Kamal_
From : Japanese Language Institute
Date : _June 25, 1990_

In the coming quarter, you will be enrolled in :

Basic conversation 1. 2. 3. Reading 1. 2. Economic newspaper reading.
Newspaper reading. Kanji. Business conversation 1. 2.
Business preparatory, course.

Notes : 1.. Tuition (Y55,000) should be paid by _June 29 1990._
    If your tuition is not paid by the indicated date,
    your admission will be cancelled.
  2. Instruction begins on _July 3 (Tue)_
  3. Class hour : 6:10 p.m. - 8:00 p.m. (Mon, Tue, Wed, Thu)
  4. Office hour : 9:00 a.m. - 7:00 p.m. Mon - Fri.
    Closed on Sat, Sun, and National holidays.

                        INTERNATIONAL EDUCATION CENTER
                        JAPANESE LANGUAGE INSTITUTE
                            Phone : 359-9621

Sinha Kamal 様

貴方は日本語研修所夜間コースにおいて、下記のクラスに配置されましたので
お知らせいたします。

          基礎会話 1、 2、 3、 読解 1、 2、 中級準備
クラス : 漢字、 一般新聞、 経済新聞、 ビジネス会話 1、 2、

注意事項: 1、 授業料（¥55．000）を _6月29日_までにお支払下さい。
          何の御連絡も無く、指定の期日までにお支払がない場合は入学
          できません。
      2、 授業は _7月3_ 日から開始されます。
      3、 授業時間は午後6時10分から8時まで。
                    （ 月、 火、 水、 木 ）
      4、 日本語研修所の業務取り扱い時間は午前9時から午後7時まで
          です。（ 月曜～金曜 ）

                            1990年 6月 25日
                            財団法人 国際教育振興会
                                日本語研修所
                            TEL． 359-9621

Exhibit K1: Attended a language school in Shinjuku. Self-paid.

Exhibit K1

	02	カ（ユ ヘ の日本部　　　　ハセツ（ノ）ブ	¥	2,000
	03	nihongo notes 2	¥	1,000
	04	A Course in Modern Japanese — Volume Two	¥	2,369
	05	総合日本語 ― 初級から中級へ	¥	2,800
	06	日本語いろいろ2	¥	1,400
	07	日本語中級1	¥	1,400
	08	日本語実力養成問題集	¥	1,340
	09	オフスの日本語	¥	1,700
	10	語彙	¥	950
	11	表記	¥	1,300
	12	Remembering the KATAKANA	¥	566
	13	中級からの日本語	¥	2,060
	14	Reading Japanese Financial Newspapers	¥	3,800
	15	にほんごのきそ1	¥	1,850
	16	日本語テスト問題集	¥	1,300
	17	総合 日本語中級 前期	¥	2,800
	18	日本語ジャーナル 6月1990	¥	600
	19	日本語ジャーナル 10月1990	¥	600
	20	日本語ジャーナル 11月1990	¥	600
	21	日本語ジャーナル 1月1991	¥	600
	22	ひらがなタイムズ 10月1989	¥	200
	23	ひらがなタイムズ 6月1990	¥	200
	24	NHKスタンダード日本語講座 8-9月1991	¥	500
	25	NHKスタンダード日本語講座 10-11月1991	¥	500
	26	NHKスタンダード日本語講座 12-1月1991	¥	500
	27	漢字の本 1年生	¥	800
	28	漢字の本 2年生	¥	600
	29	漢字の本 3年生	¥	600
	30	似た言葉 ― 使い分け辞典	¥	2,300
	31	故事ことわざ辞典	¥	1,340
	32	Remembering the HIRAGANA	¥	566
	33	Basic Kanji Book Vol. 1	¥	2,400
	34	3級問題集 日本語能力試験対策用	¥	1,800
	35	A New Dictionary of Kanji Usage	¥	4,940
	37	日本語分野別重要単語1500	¥	1,300
	38	現代日本語コース中級II Vol.4	¥	2,575
	39	総合日本語初級から中級へ チープ	¥	6,000
	40	Japanese:The Spoken Language 1 カセットテープ	¥	15,000
	41	Japanese:The Spoken Language 2 カセットテープ	¥	15,000
	42	Japanese:The Spoken Language 3 カセットテープ	¥	15,500
	43	Japanese:The Spoken Language 1	¥	3,200
	44	Japanese:The Spoken Language 2	¥	3,200
	45	Japanese:The Spoken Language 3	¥	3,300
	46	日本語初歩	¥	1,900
	47	日本語初歩 カセットテープ	¥	7,004
	48	現代日本語コース中級II 聴解ワークシート	¥	5,000

Exhibit K2: A partial list of books and tapes I bought to learn Japanese-language.

Exhibit K2

Student Report

NAME **MR. SINHA, Kamal**   LANGUAGE Japanese   DATE 2nd October, 1989

NO. & TYPE OF LESSONS (on 2~   tember, '89 at Yokohama-Nishiguchi Japanese Center

LEVELS

A	INTERNATIONAL EXECUTIVE / 国際業務レベル I	
B	INTERNATIONAL BUSINESS / 国際業務レベル II	
C	BASIC BUSINESS / 基礎業務レベル	
D	BASIC FLUENCY / 一般・日常レベル	**F+**
E	SOCIAL / 基礎レベル	実用評価
F	ELEMENTARY / 入門レベル	

REMARKS

		EXCELLENT	GOOD	AVERAGE	FAIR	WEAK
1.	PROGRESS / 進度					
2.	COMPREHENSION / 理解力		X			
3.	FLUENCY / 会話力			X		
4.	GRAMMAR / 文法			X		
5.	VOCABULARY / 語彙			X		
6.	RETENTION / 記憶力					
7.	PRONUNCIATION / 発音			X		
8.	PARTICIPATION / 参加度		X			
9.	RAPPORT / 意欲			X		
10.	CONFIDENCE / 自信			X		
11.	ATTENDANCE / 出席率					
12.	POTENTIAL / 可能性	X				

The remarks ratings refer to the degree of proficiency between levels within the indicated level ⑫ 各項目の REMARKS は指示されたレベル内 ⑫ における区分です

COMMENTS

Mr. Kamal Sinha seemed to have little knowledge of grammar and its usage, although he has some basic vocabulary. His listening comprehension seems to be somewhat stronger than that speaking fluency. His speech is too broken for even for a short conversation, and he is able to answer simple questions only using words instead of complete sentences. He appeared to be a very enthusiastic and keen student, and he adapted himself to the Berlitz Method quite smoothly during his trial lesson. Overall performance indicates the need for thorough drilling of basic grammar before proceeding to intermediate and advanced sentence structures. Also, specific attention should be given to vocabulary acquisition, as well as correct usage of grammar. Considering his present level and his vocabulary, we anticipate that he will need approximately 90 to 120 private lessons to reach Social Level "E", in which he would be able to converse comfortably on simple daily topics. And an additional 120 to 150 lessons will be required for him in order to cover all the grammatical structures and vocabulary necessary to function at the BAsic Fluency Level "D", which will enable him to communicate accurately in general situations and some simple business

Exhibit L1: Berlitz's F+ detailed evaluation of my business Japanese.

Exhibit L1

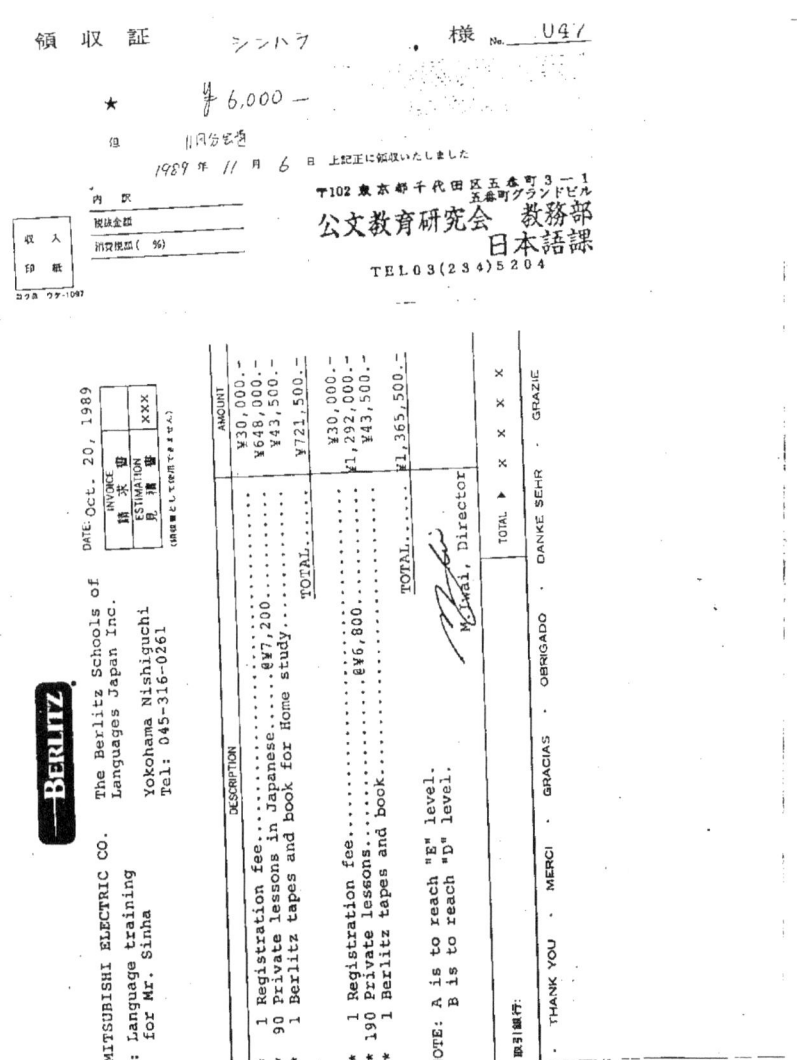

MITSUBISHI ELECTRIC CO.

The Berlitz Schools of
Languages Japan Inc.

le: Language training
for Mr. Sinha

Yokohama Nishiguchi
Tel: 045-316-0261

DATE: Oct. 20, 1989

請求書　INVOICE
見積書　ESTIMATION

(消費税として（但月として利ます税）)

DESCRIPTION		AMOUNT
* 1 Registration fee....................		¥30,000.−
* 90 Private lessons in Japanese.....@¥7,200		¥648,000.−
* 1 Berlitz tapes and book for Home study...		¥43,500.−
TOTAL.....		¥721,500.−
* 1 Registration fee....................		¥30,000.−
* 190 Private lessons.............@¥6,800.		¥1,292,000.−
* 1 Berlitz tapes and book............		¥43,500.−
TOTAL.....		¥1,365,500.−

M. Imai, Director

NOTE: A is to reach "E" level.
B is to reach "D" level.

取引銀行:

	TOTAL ▶	×	×	×

THANK YOU　・　MERCI　・　GRACIAS　・　OBRIGADO　・　DANKE SEHR　・　GRAZIE

Exhibit L2: Berlitz's cost estimates. 1.4 million yens to read a D level in Japanese.

Exhibit L2

Certificate

Mitsubishi Electric Test of English Proficiency

Hereby Awarded to

MITSUBISHI ELECTRIC CORPORATION
Personnel Affairs & Labor Relations Dept.

Exhibit M: Result of English proficiency evaluation for Mitsubishi Electric.

Exhibit M

財団法人 日本国際教育協会
理事長 逸見博昌
Hiromasa Hemmi, President
Association of International Education, Japan

国際交流基金
理事長 服部新
Shinichiro Asao, President
The Japan Foundation

日本語能力試験（平成 4 年 12 月実施 ）の成績を次の通り通知します。
Your scores of the Japanese-Language Proficiency Test given in December, 1992 are listed as follows.

級 Level	合 格 PASSED	受 験 番 号 Application Number
1	PASSED	1107312

氏　　名 Name	性 別 Sex	生 年 月 日 Date of Birth	国・地域 Country or Region
SINHA, KAMAL	男		インド

注： 一部の科目しか受験しなかった者の当該科目欄
及び総合点には「＊」で付してある。

文字・語彙 Writing & Vocabulary	聴 解 Listening	読解・文法 Reading & Grammar	総 合 点 Total Score
8 8 /100	8 0 /100	1 8 1 /200	3 0 9 /400

Association of International Education, Japan and The Japan Foundation administer this Japanese Language Proficiency Test for the measurement and certification of Japanese language proficiency for non-native speakers both in Japan and abroad.

Those certified in this test are attained to possess an ability equivalent to the criteria at each level given below:

Level 1: The examinee should have mastered grammar at a high level, about 2,000 Kanji and 10,000 vocabulary words, and have an integrated command of the language sufficient for life in Japanese society and providing a useful base for study at a Japanese university. This level should be reached after studying Japanese for about 900 hours.

Level 2: The examinee should have mastered grammar at a relatively high level, about 1,000 Kanji and 6,000 vocabulary words, and have the ability to converse, read and write about matters of a general nature. This level should be reached after studying Japanese for about 600 hours and finishing the intermediate course.

Level 3: The examinee should have mastered basic grammar, about 300 Kanji and 1,500 vocabulary words, and have the ability to take part in everyday conversation and to read and write simple sentences. This level should be reached after studying Japanese for about 300 hours and finishing the elementary course.

Level 4: The examinee should have mastered the elements of grammar, about 100 Kanji and 800 vocabulary words, and have the ability to engage in simple conversation and to read and write short, simple sentences. This level should be reached after studying Japanese for about 150 hours and finishing the first half of the elementary course.

Exhibit N: Result of my Japanese Language Proficiency Test Level 1 after three years in Japan.

Exhibit N

シンハ・カマル氏に聞く

● 三菱電機人種差別訴訟 ●

人種差別に対する慰謝料を求める

インタビュー 関口千恵

コンピュータ技術者に応募

Exhibit O: My interview by Nihon Hogaku magazine, Japan's only law review t

Exhibit O

82

Mitsubishi sued for discrimination

A 34-year-old engineer from India has filed a ¥6 million lawsuit against his former employer, Mitsubishi Electric Corp., claiming the company discriminated against him.

In his suit filed with the Tokyo District Court Tuesday, Kamal Sinha said he left a position as assistant professor at Tennessee University in the United States to join the company in September 1989 to develop data base systems.

He said he asked Mitsubishi to pay for Japanese lessons for him, since the company provided free English-language courses for its Japanese employees.

He insisted that Mitsubishi employees from the U.S. and Europe are provided an opportunity to learn Japanese.

Mitsubishi refused his request and one year after joining the company, he said, he was removed from his post because of poor Japanese lan-

KAMAL SINHA, 34, talks to reporters Tuesday after filing a lawsuit against his former employer, Mitsubishi Electric Corp., claiming he was the victim of discrimination.

guage skills.

Sinha claimed in his lawsuit his boss urged him to quit and deprived him of the chance to attend staff meetings.

"I heard that Japanese companies are more humane than those of Europe or the U.S.," Sinha said at a news conference. "But actually I

was discriminated against and harassed by my boss."

A Mitsubishi spokesman said a language barrier may have brought about misunderstanding.

But he said it was company policy not to comment on the issue until facts could be confirmed.

ndian Sues Firm 'or Race Bias

An Indian computer specialist working .r Mitsubishi Electric Corp. filed a suit 'uesday against the company in the 'okyo District Court, alleging that he is . victim of racial discrimination.

Sinha Kamal, 34, is demanding about 5.88 million in damages from Mitsubishi, .ccording to the suit.

Kamal said he was not permitted to take ree company classes in Japanese offered o other foreign employees who were .uropean and U.S. Caucasians.

.A former assistant professor of computer sc.ence at a U.S. college, Kamal said he wa. hired by Mitsubishi in 1989 as a lifet.me employee.

Whe. he began working for the company, he was .ut in charge of developing a computer .ystem, he said.

But after h. began to protest what he viewed as disc.iminatory practices at the company, he .as not given anything to do, according to .he suit.

According to the suit, supervisors told him to leave the company since he was only temporarily employed and to vacate a company condominium as soon as possible.

But a Mitsubishi public relations official, when asked about the suit, voiced a different opinion.

Daily Yomiuri, July 23, 1992 pg 2

Also covered by Asahi Evening News, Nihon Keizai, Kyodo wire, etc.

Exhibit P: Some press coverage.

Exhibit P

LUNCH MENU
APR. 16—MAY. 15, 1992

DATE	MENU
4/ 16 THU	PORK CURRY, MACARONI SALAD,
17 FRI	GRILLED MACKEREL, MEAT BALL, BOILED RADISH WITH SOY SAUCE
20 MON	CUTLET, BOILED VEGITABLE, MIXED KIDNEY BEAN WITH SESAMI
21 TUE	GRILLED SALMON, SHRIMP CREAM COROQUETTE, BOILED SEAWEAD
22 WED	FRIED CHICKEN WITH MISO, OMELETTE, LOTUS ROOTS SALAD
23 THU	GRILLED & BOILED FISH, TOMATO, CHINESE SOURED SALAD
24 FRI	=*=SPECIAL LUNCH FOR KAMADEN 30TH ANNIVERSARY=*=
27 MON	FRIED CHICKEN WITH SOYSAUCE, POTATO SALAD, BOILED SHRIMP & CORN
28 TUE	FRIED HUM CREAM, FISH CAKE, BOILED BEEF
5/ 6 WED	HAMBURG, MIXED BEAN ROOTS & NUTS, BOILED BAMBOO SHOOT
7 THU	GRILLED HORCE MACKEREL, SPRING ROLL, BOILED SEAWEAD
8 FRI	FRIED PORK & VEGITABLE, HUM & CHEESE
9 SAT	FIRED FISH WITH SESAMI, CHINESE CHICKEN SALAD, SAUSAGE
11 MON	GRILLED CHICKEN WITH MISO, LIYONAISE POTATO, BURDOCK SALAD
12 TUE	GRILLED SALMON, ONION TEMPURA, MIXED STRING BEAN & VEGITABLE
13 WED	FRIED SCALLOP CREAM, TUNA SALAD, SUKIYAKI
14 THU	FRIED & BOILED SARDINE, OMELETTE, MIXED GREEN

DATE	MENU
9/16 WED	CRAB CREAM COROQUETTE, BAKED EGG
17 THU	GRILLED SALMON, HAM & KIDNEY BEAN TENPURA, CHECKEN & EGG
18 FRI	MINCHED PORK CUTLETTE, BOILED RADISH, SASAKAMA
19 SAT	FRIED SQUID, OMELETTE, BOILED SEAWEED
21 MON	FRIED & BOILED MACKEREL, MEATBALL, BERDOCK SALAD
22 TUE	YAKINIKU(GRELLED PORK), TOMATO, SOUHED CRAB FLAKE
24 THU	FRIED BEEF & KIDNEY BEANS, MEATBALL, FRIED CARROT CREAM
25 FRI	FRIED FISH WITH SESAMI, JAPANESE PIZZA, FRIED VEGITABLE
28 MON	POTATO COROQUETTE, OMELETTE, MACARONI SALAD
29 TUE	SUKIYAKI, UNOHANA
30 WED	GRILLED FISH, BEEFUN SAUTE, ONION SALAD
10/ 1 THU	FRIED HAM CREAM, SMALL SHRIMP PATE, MABO-TOUFU
2 FRI	FRIED CHICKEN, YAKISOBA, SOURED CUCUMBER & SEAWEED
5 MON	VICTORIAN CUTLETTE, MIXED BEAN ROOTS & NUTS
6 TUE	BEEF SPRING ROLL, BOILED CARROT WITH MEAT

Exhibit Q: Lunch menu at Mitsubishi Electric.

Exhibit Q

TEST DATE							
Month	Year	Verbal				Total	
JAN	83	47	99	49	99	750	99
OCT	80	38	89	56	99	730	99

Exhibit R: GMAT Verbal score of 99%.

Exhibit R

University of Illinois at Urbana-Champaign

COLLEGE OF COMMERCE AND BUSINESS ADMINISTRATION
DEPARTMENT OF BUSINESS ADMINISTRATION · 350 COMMERCE BUILDING (WEST)
1206 S. SIXTH ST., CHAMPAIGN, ILLINOIS 61820 · (217) 333-4240

March 11, 1982

Mr. Kamal Sinha
#46 Ptolomey Towers
504 S. Rawlings St.
Carbondale, IL 62901

Dear Mr. Sinha:

Your application for admission to the Ph.D. program in Management Science
has been reviewed and we are happy to advise you that we are recommending
to the Graduate College that you be admitted as of Fall 1982. In addition,
we can offer you financial assistance in the form of a half-time graduate
assistantship and tuition and fee waiver for 1982-83.

Exhibit S1(top): Admission letter from University of Illinois, Urbana-Champaign's PhD program.
Exhibit S2 bottom): Summer 1982 Grade Report. 3 courses are listed. Assembler course not listed.

Exhibits S1 and S2

FEBRUARY 1988

ACTUARIAL EXAMINATION RESULTS

The scale of grades runs from 0 to 10. Passing grades are 6 through 10. A grade of 0 does not mean that the candidate received no credit but that he/she had a poor paper. Similarly, a grade of 10 indicates a very fine paper but not necessarily a perfect one.

COURSE	GRADE
100	10

ID#10440174   Cand#00286

SOCIETY OF ACTUARIES

560 PARK BOULEVARD, ITASCA, ILLINOIS 60143 U.S.A.
(312) 773-3010

MAY 1988

ACTUARIAL EXAMINATION RESULTS

The scale of grades runs from 0 to 10. Passing grades are 6 through 10. A grade of 0 does not mean that the candidate received no credit but that he/she had a poor paper. Similarly, a grade of 10 indicates a very fine paper but not necessarily a perfect one.

COURSE	GRADE
110	09

ID#10440174   Cand#10370

SOCIETY OF ACTUARIES

475 N. Martingale Rd
(312) 706-3500
Schaumburg, IL 60173
NOVEMBER 1988

ACTUARIAL EXAMINATION RESULTS

The scale of grades runs from 0 to 10. Passing grades are 6 through 10. A grade of 0 does not mean that the candidate received no credit but that he/she had a very poor paper. Similarly, a grade of 10 indicates a very fine paper but not necessarily a perfect one.

COURSE	GRADE
120	09
130	10
140	08
151	09

ID#10440174   Cand#01720

SINHA,KAMAL
E-13 UNIVERSITY COURTS
MARTIN   TN 38237

SOCIETY OF ACTUARIES

475 NORTH MARTINGALE ROAD, SCHAUMBURG, ILLINOIS 60173 U.S.A.
(708) 706-3500

NOVEMBER 1989
ACTUARIAL EXAMINATION RESULTS

The scale of grades runs from 0 to 10. Passing grades are 6 through 10. A grade of 0 does not mean that the candidate received no credit but that he/she had a very poor paper. Similarly, a grade of 10 indicates a very fine paper but not necessarily a perfect one.

COURSE	GRADE
150	08
220	09

ID#10440174   Cand#08208

SINHA,KAMAL
1-105 FUJIZUKA APTS
418-5 TERABUN
KAMAKURA   JAPAN
247

Exhibit T: Actuarial test scores

Exhibit T

COLLEGE FOR FINANCIAL PLANNING

Office of the President

June 30, 1989

KAMAL SINHA   87061509
E-13 UNIVERSITY COURTS
MARTIN, TN 38237

Dear Mr. Sinha:

Congratulations! You have successfully completed the Certified
Financial Planner Professional Education Program. This is a
significant accomplishment for which you should be proud.

Association
for Investment
Management
and Research

5 Boar's Head Lane
Post Office Box 3668
Charlottesville, VA 22903
Telephone: (804) 977-6600
Fax: (804) 977-1103

September 21, 1990

AIMR

135566
Kamal Sinha
Mitsubishi Electric Corp.,
Japan
System Architecture Dev.
325 Kamimachiya
Kamakura 247 Japan

Dear Mr. Sinha:

Congratulations! On September 20, 1990, the Board of Trustees approved the award of the CFA
Charter to you and 1,359 other Level III candidates.

Exhibit U: CFA and CFP progress.

Exhibit U

Index of Names

www.ingramcontent.com/pod-product-compliance
Lightning Source LLC
Chambersburg PA
CBHW060402190526
45169CB00002B/712